ARMAGEDDON AROUND THE CORNER

By the same author

SEPARATED BRETHREN

CHRISTIANITY AND AMERICAN FREEMASONRY

CHRISTIAN FAMILY FINANCE

CATHOLICS ON CAMPUS

Armageddon Around the Corner

A REPORT ON JEHOVAH'S WITNESSES

William J. Whalen

ILLUSTRATED

THE JOHN DAY COMPANY, NEW YORK

 Published by The John Day Company, 62 West 45th Street, New York 36, N.Y., and simultaneously in Canada by Longmans Canada Limited, Toronto.

Library of Congress Catalogue Card Number: 62-10958

Manufactured in the United States of America

NIHIL OBSTAT:
Edwin G. Kaiser, C.PP.S.
Censor Deputatus

IMPRIMATUR:
† John J. Carberry, D.D.
Bishop of Lafayette in Indiana
September 24, 1961

Preface

Of the three major indigenous religious movements in this country—Mormonism, Christian Science, and Jehovah's Witnesses—only the third has been more or less neglected by students of the American religious scene. Not more than a handful of studies, mostly partisan, have examined Jehovah's Witnesses as a religious and sociological phenomenon although this cult, the youngest and smallest of the three, lays claim to being the fastest-growing religion in the world.

The growth of Jehovah's Witnesses should be of interest not only to the clergy and members of the traditional churches but also to sociologists, lawyers, psychologists, mass communicators. The Brooklyn-based cult has something to tell each.

The best recent study of the Witnesses is unfortunately not available in English translation. It was written by a French Canadian Jesuit, Fr. Gérard Hébert, and published in Montreal under the title *Les Témoins de Jéhovah.* One of the rare objective studies in English was a slim book by Royston Pike. When a Knoxville, Tennessee, building contractor wrote a laudatory account of the cult he collected a portfolio of rejection slips from leading publishers until he finally turned to a vanity publisher. To the amazement of the book trade Marley Cole's *Jehovah's Witnesses: The New World Society* sold 100,000 copies the first year and ended among the top ten best sellers for 1955. His book was recommended in the pages of the *Watchtower* and by speakers at district and regional assemblies of Witnesses. Presumably many Witnesses bought the book. A sequel by the same author, *Triumphant Kingdom,* was issued two years later by another vanity publisher but failed to achieve the success of the first book.

The two Cole books and another book written by a veteran Witness, A. H. Macmillan (*Faith on the March*) are examples of favorable treatments published by non-Witness presses. On the other hand a number of Protestant ministers have written books and tracts exposing what they believe to be the unscriptural basis of the cult. The best example of books in this category is *Jehovah of the Watchtower: A Complete Exposé of Jehovah's Witnesses* by Walter R. Martin and Norman H. Klann, both Baptist ministers. Their book has gone into its fifth printing. Finally there are the two exposés by a disaffected ex-Witness, William J. Schnell, called *Thirty Years a Watch Tower Slave* and *Into the Light of Christianity*. Schnell makes his main appeal to evangelical Christians and urges them to combat Witness witnessing.

Two published Ph.D. theses have appeared. One, in abbreviated form, was published by the Yale University Press in 1933: *The International Bible Students* by Milton Stacey Czatt. The other was written by the present Dean of Students at Brooklyn College, Herbert H. Stroup, and published by the Columbia University Press in 1945 under the title *The*

Jehovah's Witnesses. Both were excellent pieces of scholarly research although the Czatt study is now somewhat dated. Considering the expansion and impact of the cult, the available secondary source material is small.

On the other hand, the researcher finds himself overwhelmed by the printed output of the Watchtower Society. J. F. Rutherford, the Society's second president, wrote 22 full-length books and dozens of pamphlets and tracts. The flow of books, magazines and tracts has not abated since his death in 1942. Since then the Watchtower has released 15 more official texts. Of course, a writer cannot rely only on such material. He must also employ observation, interviews, correspondence, etc.

My aim has been to produce neither a whitewash nor an attack on Jehovah's Witnesses. Skeletons in Watchtower closets will be rattled but accomplishments will not go unrecognized. I should make it clear that I am not a Jehovah's Witness but a Roman Catholic layman. My chief purpose is not to produce a point-by-point refutation of Watchtower doctrines on Biblical or theological grounds. Others more qualified than I as theologians may undertake this task if they wish. In fact, Father Hébert and the Rev. Messrs. Martin and Klann already have.

Inconsistencies in this book in the words "Watchtower" and "Witnesses" are carried over from the cult's own usage. It has employed at various times both "Watch Tower" and "Watchtower," and my effort has been to make in each case the choice appropriate to the time and place. For reasons of their own, cult members never capitalize "witnesses"; when quoting from their publications I follow this style, but otherwise I use the capital, as does everyone except members.

Several people have been kind enough to review the manuscript and offer valuable comments and insights. I would like to thank Father Hébert, Professor Emeritus Charles S. Braden of Northwestern University, Rev. Edwin G. Kaiser, C.PP.S., and my colleague Mr. Richard L. Pierce. It goes without saying that they do not necessarily agree with every statement I make nor should they be held responsible for my errors.

Finally, I should like to thank my wife for her patience, encouragement, and suggestions.

W.J.W.

Lafayette, Indiana

January 22, 1962

Contents

Illustrations

(all following page 96)

Nathan H. Knorr, who has headed the Witnesses of Jehovah since 1942 and has seen membership increase 800 per cent since then.

Mystery writer Mickey Spillane conducts a home Bible class shortly after his conversion to Jehovah's Witnesses in 1952.

The average Witness puts in about ten hours a month in door-to-door preaching or street-corner sales of Watchtower publications.

Baptism by immersion symbolizes the member's dedication to Jehovah.

Witnesses held the largest mass baptism in history at Orchard Beach in the Bronx during the 1958 assembly.

ARMAGEDDON AROUND THE CORNER

Come, let us make a muster speedily:
Doomsday is near; die all, die merrily.
—William Shakespeare, *Henry IV*

1. *Who Are Jehovah's Witnesses?*

CHANCES ARE at least three people call at your home year after year: the tax assessor, the Fuller Brush man, and a Witness of Jehovah. The Witness considers his "product" far more important than the life insurance, brushes or pots and pans of other doorstep salesmen. What he offers householders is nothing less than the opportunity to live through the impending battle of Armageddon and help repopulate the New World.

This climactic battle between good and evil, Jehovah God and Satan, may begin at any moment. The Witness "publisher" has no time to fritter away on unnecessary secular pursuits. The trumpet may sound before you finish reading this page. In an hour the battle may be raging.

The urgency of this message, the thoroughness of the members' indoctrination, and the shrewd direction of the organization from Brooklyn headquarters combine to explain the cult's phenomenal growth in recent years. It is the world's fastest-growing religion.

In 1942 when Judge Rutherford died and the present administration assumed direction of Jehovah's Witnesses, the cult reported about 106,000 members; in 1962 it reported more than 884,000 members around the world for a gain of 700 per cent. During the same period the 256 churches and sects in the United States failed to even double their constituencies and yet we were said to be experiencing a religious revival. Of the Witness total, approximately 250,000 are U. S. citizens. They are concentrated in the northeastern states and the West Coast.

Highest ratio of Witnesses to the general population is found in Oregon where it stands at 1 to 354. Lowest ratio is in Rhode Island, a predominately Roman Catholic state, where it is 1 Witness to 1,244 non-Witnesses. New York City now supports 108 congregations while Chicago has 44. In a number of Southern states the Watchtower Society has organized separate white and Negro Kingdom Halls.

All of these men and women consider themselves, and are considered by the parent Watchtower Bible and Tract Society, to be ordained ministers of the gospel and not just lay members. These are the trained, baptized, fully committed Witnesses who have cut their ties to the secular community and spend all their spare hours preaching the Watchtower message. They may preach, teach and baptize as ministers. They far outnumber the world-wide army of Roman Catholic priests and comprise a group several times larger than all the Protestant ministers in the United States.

Each Witness works an assigned territory and tries to make several calls a year on every household in his area. He probably calls on at least ten homes a week. Here is where he does his preaching rather than in a pulpit or before an altar. All his hours of doorstep preaching, the return or back calls he makes on interested prospects, the home Bible studies he organizes, are carefully tabulated in his local Kingdom Hall and reported periodically to Brooklyn headquarters. Last year the total hours of such door-to-door witnessing and other types of proselytizing reached a staggering 132,000,000 hours.

To sustain interest in his message of impending disaster for this old world the Witness tries to put copies of Watchtower books or magazines into the hands of all those he contacts. In Watchtower parlance he is known as a "publisher." He gets his literature at a small discount and must dispose of a quota each month but most Witnesses lose money on the transaction since they give away many publications to those who cannot afford to make a donation.

Besides this inner core of more than 875,000 publishers, the New World movement can count hundreds of thousands more who read Watchtower books, subscribe to *Watchtower* and *Awake!*, meet in Bible study groups, attend public meetings in Kingdom Halls, and generally sympathize with the doctrines and customs of Jehovah's Witnesses. These thousands may be advancing in the lengthy indoctrination leading to full membership but since they have not yet asked for baptism they do not appear on the Society's records.

The circulation of Watchtower publications puts all other religious periodicals in the shade. Every year the Society prints, binds and sells more than 5,000,000 books and Bibles in dozens of languages; the usual contribution asked varies from 50 cents to 75 cents. In religious publishing circles a title which sells more than 25,000 copies breaks into the best seller ranks; the Watchtower's basic doctrinal exposition *Let God Be True* was issued in a first edition of 10,000,000 copies in 1946. To date more than 17,000,000 copies of this 320-page book have been distributed.

Every two weeks 3,900,000 copies of the *Watchtower* magazine in 61 languages roll off the Society's rotary presses. Another 3,400,000 copies of the companion *Awake!* appear in 23 languages. Both journals sell for only five cents a copy and carry no ads. In comparison the largest Roman Catholic monthly counts only a few more than 1,000,000 subscribers and these get the magazine as part of their Knights of Columbus dues. Only ten U. S. magazines have more subscribers than the *Watchtower*.

No cult of comparable size enjoys the visibility of Jehovah's Witnesses. Few homes escape the regular calls of the indefatigable Witness missionary. Few business districts lack a contingent of Witnesses with magazine bags and handbills. Most of the larger cities in the country have played host to Witness assemblies. At the 1958 international Divine Will Assembly in New York City more than 253,000 men, women and children jammed into the Polo Grounds and Yankee Stadium for the final Sunday afternoon rally. Witnesses boast that this was the largest religious gathering in modern times. (Catholics say that more than 1,000,000 people attended the closing meeting of the International Eucharistic Congress in Munich on August 7, 1960.)

Claiming only the rights of aliens in all countries in which they live, the Witnesses refuse to vote, serve in the military forces, salute the flag, hold public office, participate in civic affairs. They have been tarred and feathered in a dozen American communities, tortured and gassed in Hitler's concentration camps, banned in fascist Spain, driven underground by the Communists in Soviet Russia and the satellites. In the United States only the Mormons suffered more for their faith and that was more than a century ago. In proportion to their numbers, only the Jews have counted more martyrs during this century than Jehovah's Witnesses.

Neither pacifists nor conscientious objectors, thousands of Witnesses in the United States refused to register for the draft during World War II or to report for induction. They raise no objection to war and slaughter and almost relish the contemplation of Armageddon's carnage but they claim to obey only Jehovah as commander in chief in any holy war. And He has excused His Witnesses from fighting at Armageddon. They balk at nonmilitary service in work camps and hospitals since they claim the rights of aliens not citizens. More than 7,000 spent time in federal prisons for their convictions in the last war.

Officials of the American Civil Liberties Union state that no group in the history of the nation has done more to advance the cause of civil liberties than the Witnesses. Following a fixed policy of appealing every adverse decision, Witness lawyers carried more than 50 cases to the Supreme Court and won two-thirds of them. Most of these decisions were handed down between 1935 and 1945 when the nation was in no mood to coddle a minority of obstreperous religious fanatics who pestered religious people, cursed the orthodox churches, dodged the draft and refused to salute the flag. Nevertheless by these significant Supreme Court decisions all Americans have had their rights spelled out in such matters as selling religious tracts without a license, calling on householders who may not wish to be bothered, saluting the flag, holding religious meetings and parades, and so on.

Dissatisfied with the available Bible translations, the Witnesses set about to provide a modern English translation of their own. Discarding the terms Old Testament and New Testament they have produced a curious version known as the New World Translation of the Hebrew Scriptures and the Christian Greek Scriptures in six volumes. Among many changes they substitute "Jehovah" for the "Lord" and "God" of standard versions. Now they still use Protestant and Catholic translations to persuade prospective converts, rely on their own New World version for Kingdom Hall and private Bible study.

Witnesses are "agin" a litany of things: blood transfusions, Catholicism, commerce, Christmas trees, Communism, civic enterprises, the doctrines of hell and immortality, evolution, flag saluting, higher education, hunting and fishing, labor unions, liquor, lodges, Protestantism, priests, the Pope, military service, ministers, movies, Mother's Day, religion, Sunday schools, the Trinity, tobacco, the United Nations, voting, the YMCA, Wall Street, etc., etc. Witnesses try to isolate themselves and their families from all contamination by the world, Satan's world.

Some readers may remember the Witness missionary of Judge Rutherford's day—usually an ornery, self-righteous, fiery-eyed sort who tramped around on Sunday mornings with his phonograph and assortment of the Judge's recorded sermonettes. To those who would not listen he had nothing but contempt and dire warnings. He and his fellows won what a *Saturday Evening Post* writer termed a reputation for "conscientious cussedness on a grand scale."

Since the Judge's passing the cult has undergone a thorough public relations face lifting. Today's Witness smiles, chucks baby under the chin, pets Fido, and absorbs insults and indifference with a certain graciousness. You are not interested? he thinks. No mind. I'll be back in six months or another of the brothers or sisters will work my route. The cult substituted honey for vinegar; its membership charts attest to the attraction of honey.

Nerve center for the booming world-wide movement is a

complex of buildings facing the East River in Brooklyn. At the 11-story Bethel Home more than 650 men and women live and labor for the New World Society, for which they receive room, board and $14 a month allowance. They write the books and articles, set the type, run the presses, fill the orders, answer the mail, and work with the officers directing and supplying the needs of the cult now spread to 170 nations, islands and territories.

Here and in similar Bethels in the 85 branches around the globe the full-time workers publish literature in 146 languages and contribute the skilled labor which enables the cult to offer bound books at nominal cost. Everyone lives on the same standard, from President Nathan Homer Knorr to the newest recruit.

Through the centuries from the first Christians to the latest Southern California crank, there have been those who felt impelled to warn mankind that it was living in the latter days and that it must prepare for the looming Götterdämmerung. Thousands of Christians expected the end of things to come in the year 1000 A.D. In recent years William Miller stirred up his followers with his predictions of the Second Coming in 1843 and 1844. He started the movement which was taken over by others and turned into the aggressive Seventh-day Adventist church.

When Joseph Smith founded the Mormon church the name he picked emphasized his belief that mankind was nearing the end of its trail. He called it the Church of Jesus Christ of Latter-day Saints and stressed the urgency of the Saints gathering at Zion to await the start of the millennium. That eschatological hope gets little attention in present-day Mormonism.

Even such a rascal as Benjamin Purnell of the House of David held the reins on his community by claiming to be able to set—and reset—the date for the Second Coming. He died before he could stand trial on charges of seducing 22 girls in the Benton Harbor colony.

In these perilous days when every morning's newspaper brings its expected measure of bad news, the strategists of the New World Society find a growing acceptance of their analysis and answer. Once they and such groups as the Adventists stood alone predicting the end of the world. Now they find agnostic scientists, sober statesmen, journalists and churchmen warning that a world living in the shadow of the H-bomb is living in the latter days unless it can find some way to outlaw war. They call it World War III or the Last War; the Witnesses call it Armageddon, and have for 70 years.

Who has not thought about the possibility of an H-bomb holocaust, the pressure of overpopulation, widespread corruption in high office, juvenile delinquency, Communist expansion, racial violence and injustice, influence peddling, the spread of pornography and the sex-and-violence cult, dope addiction, the divorce rate and the dozens of other problems of our times and not felt at least a fleeting moment of despair? To the average man these problems seem so complex and beyond comprehension or manipulation that he may be tempted to throw up his hands in a final gesture of resignation.

At this point the Watchtower steps in and offers him a chance to resign from this wicked world and its messes. The world's wars, its politics and injustices no longer concern Jehovah's Witnesses. They are no longer a part of this world but have taken out citizenship in Jehovah's clean New World Society. The old world is past redemption. Its problems cannot be solved because Jehovah God wishes them to remain unsolved. This is Satan's world and to rule it and the majority of mankind who serve him he relies on the wicked trinity of organized religion, politics, and business. No earthly society—democratic, Communist, fascist, socialist—gives Jehovah His due and acknowledges the supremacy of the New World Society, the Theocracy. All are therefore doomed. The only concessions the true Witnesses of Jehovah will make to these societies is to pay their taxes and obey those laws which do not conflict with Jehovah's will.

Only those who decide to board the ark of the New World Society will ride through the horrors of the battle of Armageddon. Most of mankind will side with Satan and be lost, annihilated. They are the stiff-necked people who refuse to give a hearing to Jehovah's Witnesses, who remain in the apostate churches of Christendom, and who put their trust in worldly governments and in the United Nations. The Witnesses have not the slightest doubt that they serve the only organization on earth authorized to express the will of Jehovah, namely, the Watchtower Bible and Tract Society.

Despite the tens of thousands who board the ark every year few among them can be counted among the influential or prominent. More than 30 years ago Charles W. Ferguson observed: "No other sect in modern times has so completely captured the imagination of the unimaginative."[1] Hardly any college graduates join its ranks. You will find no political leaders, captains of industry, professors or generals in the New World Society. True, one lifelong Witness in Abilene, Kansas, lived to see her son head the Allied invasion of Europe. He later became President of the United States, but his political biographers preferred to say that he came from a family of River Brethren. Actually the Russellite Bible Students in Abilene met in the Eisenhower home for 20 years until the group outgrew their parlor and rented a hall.

Mr. Eisenhower served as "elder" or Bible study conductor. Mrs. Eisenhower was baptized a Russellite in 1897 and revealed in correspondence at the age of eighty-two that she still considered herself "in the truth" as a Witness of Jehovah. Another more recent convert has seen his paperback mysteries run into the millions of copies. Mickey (Mike Hammer) Spillane temporarily retired from his sex-and-sadism writing when he joined the cult nine years ago.

Should the growth of Jehovah's Witnesses continue at anywhere near the pace set during the past 30 years the cult may well become a serious threat to organized Christianity. They could easily move from the position of a minor to a major sect. They have blended elements of some of the most successful Christian heresies, notably Arianism, with a modern message to bewildered mankind. Their denial of hell no longer shocks society as it did in the 1880's when it was first preached. Their racial equality, anticolonialism, political neutralism, have so far stood them in good stead with many Africans. In a country like Northern Rhodesia one out of every 82 inhabitants is already a Witness of Jehovah. The cult's rapid spread in nominally Roman Catholic areas of Latin America has not gone unnoticed by Church authorities.

Perhaps as many as two million people already consider Kingdom Hall to be their spiritual home. By 1970 this figure may reach five million or more. Since 1950 the annual percentage of increase of publishers has been around 10 per cent. The gloomier the world scene and greater the threat of all-out nuclear war the brighter the recruitment picture for the Brooklyn-based cult.

What do Jehovah's Witnesses believe? How did they get started? How are they organized? What are their missionary methods? These and other questions we will try to answer in the following chapters. (Should Armageddon begin before you finish this book my publisher has agreed to refund its full purchase price.)

2. *Pastor Russell Turns the Hose on Hell*

For some time now, the young Allegheny, Pennsylvania, haberdasher had been drifting from the harsh Calvinism of nineteenth-century Presbyterianism. Once as a teen-ager he had felt so strongly about predestination and God's consignment of sinners to an eternal hell that he had gone about his home town chalking scriptural passages on walks and walls so that passers-by might heed the loss of their souls.

According to his own account he had engaged a pool-hall acquaintance in a debate on the existence of hell and lost. This shook his faith in the Christianity he had known and although he switched to the more liberal Congregational Church, he found himself a religious skeptic at the age of seventeen.

Charles Taze Russell was born in 1852. His mother had died when he was only nine and by the time he was fifteen he was in partnership with his father in the clothing business. He helped his father expand the family business into a five-store chain in the Allegheny-Pittsburgh area.

For three years after his disillusionment with Christianity

the young man dabbled in the study of Oriental religions. Then he came to the startling conclusion—startling for the nineteenth century—that a man could be a Christian and reject the notion of hell. He reasoned: "Would you hold a puppy dog's tail in the fire three minutes? Of course not, unless you were subhuman. Yet we are taught that God himself consigns creatures to everlasting torture in fire hotter than any we can imagine." To hell with the doctrine of hell, thought Charles T. Russell.

By accident the young man dropped into a dingy hall where an Adventist preacher, Jonas Wendall, was explaining the Second Coming of Jesus Christ to a handful of listeners. "Though his scripture exposition was not entirely clear and though it was very far from what we now rejoice in, it was sufficient, under God, to re-establish my wavering faith in the divine inspiration of the Bible, and to show that the records of the apostles and prophets are indissolubly linked," Russell later testified.

His introduction to Adventism sparked renewed interest in the Bible and he gathered a small band of Bible students together. This was in 1870. Unlike the Adventists, who generally expected the Lord to return in the flesh in 1873 or 1874 to destroy the world and the wicked, Russell decided that Christ might well return not in the flesh but in an invisible manner.

Adventism itself began when a Baptist seaman and War of 1812 veteran, William Miller, turned to the Bible to discover that the Lord was coming again in 1843 or 1844. Thousands joined his movement, leaving the Baptist, Disciples, Methodist and other churches. But when these dates came and went most of his converts fell away. A handful persisted in their belief that the end of the world was nigh. They refigured the Bible prophecies and continued to look for the final day. One of these bands of post-Miller Millerites, guided by the prophetess Ellen G. White, incorporated observance of the Saturday Sabbath and various health and dietary regulations into a church now known as the Seventh-day Adventist. Russell thought Miller had the right idea but was simply 30 years off in his calculations.

To make known his own interpretation of the invisible Second Coming, Russell published a booklet, *The Object and Manner of the Lord's Return.* His father gave him $1,000 to pay for the printing. Before his death the author would compile scriptural commentaries which would exceed 16,000,000 copies in circulation.

Two years later, on a business trip to Philadelphia, Russell happened to come across a magazine called *The Herald of the Morning* which was being published in Rochester, New York. The editor of this Adventist journal had, like Russell, concluded that Jesus had returned as an invisible angel in 1874 and that mankind was already in the early years of the millennium. Russell was delighted to see that the editor, N. H. Barbour, agreed with his own position and he arranged a meeting.

Russell agreed to pump some money into the ailing magazine. (When Russell finally sold out his interest in the clothing chain he netted more than $250,000.) Barbour, a printer by trade, would continue to put out the magazine but Russell would become co-editor.

The next year the eager co-editor called a meeting of all the Protestant ministers in the Pittsburgh area. Many accepted the invitation and Russell patiently explained his new understanding of the invisible parousia to the assembled clergymen. Some smiled, some muttered about wasting an evening; all went back to expound orthodox Christianity from their respective pulpits. One would think that even at a green twenty-five, Russell could not have seriously imagined that his distinguished clerical guests would rush to adopt his self-taught scriptural discoveries. All his life, however, he harbored the bitterest feelings toward the clergy of all denominations. Some of this bitterness can no doubt be attributed to the humiliating unveiling of his doctrine in 1877.

Russell and Barbour co-authored a 196-page book, *Three Worlds or Plan of Redemption,* in the same year. They explained the calculations which led them to believe that the Second Coming had come. The date of the coming—1874 —also marked the start of a 40-year harvest of souls which would end with the times of the Gentiles in 1914. Thoroughly wrapped up in his Biblical studies and writing, Russell now sold out his business interests and devoted all his time to writing, preaching in occasionally hospitable churches, organizing Bible study cells.

Next Russell broke with his collaborator Barbour on a technical interpretation of the ransom paid by Jesus. Although Russell continued to submit a few articles in contradiction of what he considered to be Barbour's heresies, he finally decided to break the association completely.

He launched his own magazine. In July 1879 appeared the first issue of *The Watch Tower and Herald of Christ's Presence.* The press run of this first issue was 6,000 copies; today the semimonthly *Watchtower* reports a circulation of 3,900,000 copies. Barbour's magazine soon folded and Barbour faded into obscurity.

Slowly Russell hammered out his theological system. He rummaged around the Bible for proof texts and found most of the wood and nails for his construction in the Books of

Daniel and Revelation. He saw mankind living in the last days of the long struggle between God and Satan, who has ruled the world since Adam's sin. He denied the divinity of Jesus Christ and the Christian doctrine of the Trinity. Men, said the young Bible student, do not have an immortal soul. The effect of Adam's sin of disobedience was primarily the penalty of death.

Russell's original complaint with traditional Christianity over the doctrine of hell was solved to his satisfaction when he determined that the Hebrew word *sheol* should invariably be translated as the common grave of mankind. "The Hebrew word sheol occurs 65 times in the Old Testament Scriptures. It is three times translated pit, 31 times translated grave, and 31 times translated hell. These are all faulty translations, if measured by the present general use of the words hell, grave and pit." [1]

Russell had nothing if not confidence in himself. He knew no more Hebrew, Greek or Latin than he could dig out of a bilingual dictionary but he did not hesitate to take on the leading Biblical scholars of the day and tell them they were all wrong.

Establishing that Christ had returned invisibly in 1874—at least to the satisfaction of his followers—the young, intense Russell began to direct the attention of his readers to the year 1914. He decided that the times of the Gentiles began when Nebuchadnezzar overthrew Jerusalem. Secular historians put this at 586 B.C. Russell declared it was in October, 607 B.C. Israel was to suffer "seven times" for her sins (Leviticus 26:18) so Russell had to measure the length of the Gentile times. He discovered that the Bible in one passage called 1,260 days to be 3½ times so he doubled this to get seven times. This made 2,520 days. He further determined that in these prophecies each day equals a year. He changed the 2,520 days to years, subtracted 606 (dropping November and December in 607) and finally arrived at 1914 as the date of the end of the Gentile times. To his followers this meant the end of the world as they knew it and their translation into spirit creatures and associates of Jesus.

Russell began to use the title "Pastor" which had been conferred by the many Bible study groups he shepherded. He himself never set foot in a college or seminary nor did he receive ordination by any of the established denominations, which he branded apostate religions and suburbs of Babylon.

Readers of his magazine were constantly encouraged to form study groups using the magazine as their text. By 1880 the Pastor had been chosen nominal head of about 30 groups in Pennsylvania, Ohio, New York, New Jersey, Massachusetts, Delaware and Michigan. He tried to visit each congregation personally.

These first Russellites or, as they were sometimes known, Millennial Dawnists held one communion service a year. This was in Pittsburgh. They called this the Anniversary Supper while today's Jehovah's Witnesses use the term Memorial or Evening Meal. The Pastor declared it should be observed on the exact anniversary date of the original Last Supper, Nisan 14. The annual spring communion gathering in Pittsburgh also served as a convention and get-together for the scattered Russellites.

Ties among the original Pittsburgh congregations and the small groups in the East and Middle West were loose and informal. Russell introduced and recommended the same form of church government he had known as a Congregationalist. Each group elected a board of elders for one-year terms. The Pastor made it clear that he considered this method to be the only scripturally approved form of church polity:

> Nor should any brother assume public duties in the Church as leader, representative, etc. without an election—even though assured that there is no question respecting his acceptability. The Scriptural method of ordaining elders in all the churches is by congregational election—by stretching forth the hand in vote.[2]

Russell's emphatic endorsement of democratic procedures would give his successor, Judge Rutherford, some bad times in later years when he jettisoned this system in favor of the centralized appointment of all congregational officials. Not a few old-timers would abandon the Society in the 1930's as the new autocratic methods were imposed by Brooklyn.

The Pastor urged his people to spread the glad tidings by distributing his magazine, tracts, and books such as his *Food for Thinking Christians* (1881). By 1884 he had received a state charter for a corporation called Zion's Watch Tower Tract Society, the forerunner of the present Watch Tower Bible and Tract Society of Pennsylvania, one of the three legal instrumentalities of Jehovah's Witnesses.

Outgrowing their original quarters, the mother congregation in Pittsburgh built the Bible House in 1889. The four-story building featured a 200-seat assembly hall, a small printing plant, shipping room, living quarters for headquarters personnel, editorial offices. It served as headquarters for 20 years.

Pastor Russell's first full-length book had appeared in 1886 and was called *The Divine Plan of the Ages.* Its author explained, "The testimony of modern theologians has been given no weight, and that of the so-called Early Fathers has been omitted." [3] He damned the Church of Rome and its papacy, identified as the anti-Christ, for distorting pure doctrine and discouraging private Bible study. He had only a slightly more favorable view of Protestantism. "Since their [the Reformers'] day, Protestants have made little progress because instead of walking in the light, they have halted around their favorite leaders, willing to see as much as they saw but nothing more." [4]

The Pastor waded into the Darwinian controversy which upset Christian minds in his day. He would have nothing to do with any theory of evolution.

> Surely if unintelligent nature were the creator or evolver she would continue the process, and there would be no such thing as fixed species, since without intelligence nothing would arrive at fixed conditions. Evolution would be a fact today, and we would see about us fish becoming birds, and monkeys becoming man.[5]

The Pastor told his readers that Adam and Eve were created approximately 6,000 years ago. Eventually he conceded that perhaps the creative week of Jehovah might have been 42,000 years before the appearance of the first man. This, he pointed out, was considerably more reasonable and Biblical than the "geological guesses" of millions and billions of years being discussed by agnostic and atheistic scientists.

His Arian views of the nature of Jesus were made clear in his writings. "The scriptures teach that there have been two, and only two, perfect men—Adam and Jesus." [6] He explained, "When Jesus was in the flesh he was a perfect human being; previous to that time he was a perfect spiritual being; and since his resurrection he is a perfect spiritual being of the highest or divine order." [7]

This first book was to become the first of a series of six *Studies in the Scriptures* (originally called *Millennial Dawn*) published during the Pastor's lifetime. These and a posthumous seventh volume issued shortly after his death would remain the doctrinal mainstay of the Russellites until the early 1920's. Today Jehovah's Witnesses no longer reprint the Pastor's books; rarely do you meet a Witness who shows any familiarity with Russell's life or writings. Seldom do any modern Witness writers even quote from the Pastor's voluminous literary output.

One understandable reason for letting the Pastor's books slide into practical oblivion (the original six volumes are still distributed by the schismatic Dawn Bible Students) is that these books often contradict current Witness interpretations. We have seen that Russell taught that congregational election of elders was the only scriptural form of church government whereas today all officers get their appointments from the Brooklyn Pentagon. Russell thought Jesus died on a cross; the Witnesses insist it was a torture stake without crossbar. Witnesses now refuse all military service even in noncombat roles. Pastor Russell thought that every citizen should bear arms if so required by law.[8] He discouraged his followers from voting in elections but added:

> We may be required to do military service whether we vote or not, however; and if required we would be obliged to obey the powers that be, and should consider that the Lord's providence had permitted conscription and that he was able to overrule it to the good of ourselves and others.[9]

Russell seems to know nothing about the evil of blood transfusions, the Theocracy, the "other sheep" and Jonadabs, the wickedness of saluting the flag. No wonder the

Watchtower Society deems it best not to upset sensitive souls with such unreliable testimony.

Reading the Pastor's original six volumes published between 1886 and 1904, anyone would get the impression that the author fully expected the end of the world as we know it to come in 1914 or early 1915 at the latest. He thought October 1914 would be the most probable time for Armageddon. When events did not turn out as predicted, even the Pastor had to acknowledge the hazards of doomsday prophesying. He prepared new Forewords to his *Studies* in 1916 and noted:

> Dealing with subjects so difficult that they are rarely touched by others, it is not to be considered strange if some of the suggestions made in this Volume have not been fulfilled with absolute accuracy to the very letter.[10]

In fact, to forestall any consternation on the part of his readers, the Pastor altered a number of the rather positive statements he had made in the pre-1914 editions. For example:

1908 Edition	*1916 Edition*
Some time before the end of A.D. 1914 the last member of the divinely recognized Church of Christ . . . will be glorified with the Head (II, 77).	Some time before the end of the overthrow the last member of the divinely recognized Church of Christ . . . will be glorified with the Head (II, 77).
That the deliverance of the saints must take place some time before 1914 is manifest (III, 228).	That the deliverance of the saints must take place very soon after 1914 is manifest (III, 228).

The full end of the times of the Gentiles, i.e., the full end of their lease of dominion, will be reached in A.D. 1914; and that date will be the farthest limit of the rule of imperfect men (II, 76-77).	The full end of the times of the Gentiles, i.e., the full end of their lease of dominion, will be reached in A.D. 1914; and that date will see the disintegration of the rule of imperfect men (II, 76-77).

The ethical acceptability of doctoring such predictions and at least ten others in Volumes II, III and IV will be left to the scruples of the reader. What is clear is that Russell fully expected the end of this evil world in 1914 and the beginning of the reign of Jehovah on earth. The veteran Witness of Jehovah A. H. Macmillan would write in 1957: "We expected 1914 would mark the end of this system of things on earth. Our big concern at that time was to preach as effectively and extensively as possible before that date arrived. In the meantime, we thought, we must prepare ourselves individually to be ready to go to heaven." [11]

In these and a dozen other matters Russell differed from the modern Watchtower Society so that republication of his works would only unsettle those "in the truth." He has, in fact, become something of a skeleton in the closet of the Society.

But all these later discrepancies were unknown to the readers of the *Watch Tower* in the late 1890's. Small groups in Canada and England as well as in the United States got together for Bible studies and relied mainly on Pastor Russell's magazine and tracts for spiritual nourishment. The Pastor himself visited Europe in 1891 to call on these groups and others in Ireland and Scotland. He also toured Russia, Turkey and Egypt. The Society opened its first foreign branch in 1900, in London.

Combining business and pleasure, about 360 Bible Students headed for Chicago in 1893 to attend the convention of the Society and also the World's Fair. About 70 men and women submitted to baptism by immersion.

Another embarrassment to present-day Witnesses who know anything about it is Pastor Russell's fascination with the Great Pyramid Theory. In *Thy Kingdom Come* (Volume III in the *Studies*) the Pastor devotes 70 pages complete with diagrams to his analysis of the measurements and arrangements of rooms and passages in the Great Pyramid. He called the pyramid a Bible in stone and "strong corroborative witness to God's plan."

To the *Watch Tower* editor the pyramid was "a storehouse of important truth—scientific, historic, and prophetic—and its testimony is found to be in perfect accord with the Bible expressing the prominent features of its truths in beautiful and fitting symbols." [12] Russell believed that God had so inspired the Pharaoh and his architects that they built the huge pyramid according to a secret key. Once deciphered, this key was shown to agree perfectly with Russell's own Biblical interpretations and predictions about the year 1914 A.D., the millennium, etc. "Then Jehovah will show himself a great Savior; and he has already prepared the Great Pyramid as a part of his instrumentality for convincing the world of his wisdom, foreknowledge and grace." [13]

In his addiction to Pyramidism, as this fad was known, Russell borrowed heavily from the speculations of other seers of his era. He believed "The Great Pryamid speaks to us, not by hieroglyphics, nor by sketches, but only by its location, its construction and its measurements." [14] The key to the riddle was to measure the lengths of various passages as representing the ages of mankind, using one inch to equal one year.

The Pastor thought that the building of the pyramid itself disproved the theory of evolution to the satisfaction of all but the proud and stiff-necked scientists. Putting the date of its completion at 2170 B.C. the Pastor asked how anyone could imagine that these "prehistoric" men could know enough to build the pyramid.

When the Pastor revised his books in 1916 he declared in his Preface: "The Great Pyramid of Egypt discussed in this Volume has not lost any of its interest to the author."[15] Rutherford would finally discard all references to the "corroborative evidence" of the stone Bible. Questions about the Pyramid Theory now produce nothing but blank stares from otherwise fluent Witnesses.

One feature of the Pastor's gigantic literary output was, if anything, intensified by Rutherford and continued to some extent by Knorr. This was the constant and virulent anti-Catholicism with which the Russellites and Jehovah's Witnesses have often been identified.

The Pastor usually attempted to link the papacy with the anti-Christ. In Volume III he devoted a page to his analysis of the population of England. He maintained that the nation harbored 1,500,000 Roman Catholics of whom 37,300 were in jail. Of the 7,000,000 infidels on the same island only 350 were behind bars.[16] The conclusion was obvious: better to be an infidel than a papist.

Russell appointed three full-time representatives in 1897 to visit the congregations sprouting around the country. They were known as "pilgrims." By 1905 their ranks had grown to 25 and by 1917 there were 93. The Pastor suggested that some of the faithful station themselves near Protestant churches on Sunday mornings to distribute Watch Tower tracts and books, especially his tract on the Bible *vs.* evolution.

The Pastor himself developed into a spellbinding preacher who spoke six to eight hours a day expounding his Bible teachings. He crisscrossed the continent challenging ministers to debate with him on such topics as the existence of hell. He visited many of the local congregations which had elected him their pastor in absentia. In 1903 the Pastor set up a branch office in Germany and presided at a convention in Put-in-Bay, Ohio, which attracted a reported 4,800 Bible Students.

If Russell could view the spread of his doctrines in this country and abroad with some satisfaction, he faced a grim domestic situation. He once observed that "many of the Lord's most faithful children live in a matrimonial furnace of affliction." He was speaking autobiographically.

Russell had married Maria Frances Ackley in 1879 and Mrs. Russell had been closely associated with his evangelism and editorial work. The couple had no children. After 18 years as associate editor of the *Watch Tower* Mrs. Russell began to disagree with her husband over the management of the magazine. In 1897 she packed up and left him. They lived apart for six years and Mrs. Russell filed suit for legal separation in 1903. The trial reached the jury three years later.

One complaint of the disgruntled Mrs. Russell was the Pastor's relations with an orphan girl the couple had taken into their home in 1889. Questioned about his relations with the girl, the Pastor was quoted as saying: "I am like a jellyfish. I float around here and there. I touch this one and that, and if she responds I take her to me, and if not I float on to others."

Naturally the newspapers followed the trial of the popular

preacher with avid interest. Russell was soon pegged as the "Jellyfish Pastor" and the name stuck with him to his death. For example, the *Washington Post* for May 4, 1906, commented:

The Rev. Russell says he's like a jellyfish; that he floats about, touching his lady parishioners whenever he gets near enough, and that, when they "respond,"—whatever that may mean,—he embraces. He adds that the only hell he knows of or believes in is a strictly earthly hell; from which we conclude that he finds devils only among those who do not "respond" when touched. The particular case which precipitated the divorce suit appears not to have been at all hellish. In that instance the jellyfish touched one Rose Ball, who must have "responded" very promptly, since Mrs. Maria Frances Russell, the plaintiff in the divorce suit, was an eye-witness to the embrace which followed.

But, upon the whole, this new faith, "the Russellite," seems to possess a great many of the elements of popularity. Sooner or later, of course, the higher officials of the church, and perhaps a few of the more adventurous gentlemen of the congregation, may conclude that with a little practice they might become pretty active jellyfish themselves, and that would inevitably lead to dissension. For the present, however, we are inclined to mark up the Russellite propaganda as a winner. Of course, it's a pity that the jellyfish's wife came on the scene just at the critical moment. Those accidents will occur, however, even in the most carefully arranged schemes of exaltation. The great truth remains that the Rev. Jellyfish Russell has opened up a mighty attractive pathway to the higher life, and that, barring unforeseen catastrophes, he will get there with enviable frequency.

The court legalized the separation and the judge declared that the Pastor's "course of conduct towards his wife evidences such insistent egotism and extravagant self-praise that it would be manifest to the jury that it would necessarily render the life of any sensitive Christian woman an intolerable burden."

Disputes over back alimony plagued the Pastor for several more years, until he was forced to turn over $9,000 provided by supporters to his estranged wife in 1909. She claimed he tried to avoid such payments by putting his assets into several subsidiaries of a holding company in which he held $990 of the $1,000 capital. Thousands of disillusioned Bible Students left the Society after these unsavory and sensational court actions and charges of immorality. Some followers drew the line at following a divorced preacher.

Another scandal in the movement concerned the sale of so-called Miracle Wheat. The Society began to sell bushels of Miracle Wheat at $60 a bushel or $1 a pound, promising yields at least five times as great as any known variety. Government agents testified that the wonderful wheat produced only an average yield. The Pastor countered by saying his scheme differed in no great detail from the bake sales of other churches in which possibly inferior pies were sold at exorbitant prices for the good of the work. The *Brooklyn Daily Eagle* exposed the wheat scheme and in a cartoon ridiculed Russell's claims for the seed. Russell sued for libel but lost. The pastor was ordered by the court to refund the money to Miracle Wheat buyers. Later the Pastor was found to be promoting a cancer cure which consisted of nothing but a caustic paste of chloride of zinc.

A third awkward situation for the Pastor stemmed from his constant charges that all orthodox Bible scholars were mistaken in their translations and interpretations. The Pastor larded his books with hundreds of scriptural passages and learned discussions of the correct meaning of various Greek and Hebrew words. Most people might suppose that anyone who challenged the consensus of Christian scripture scholars on major doctrines of the Bible would have some command of the original languages himself. This the self-taught Pastor did not have.

His troubles in this regard were of his own doing. He brought suit against a Baptist pastor in Hamilton, Ontario, who had written an anti-Russellite pamphlet. The writer, the Rev. J. J. Ross, branded Russell a pseudo-scholar who "never attended the higher schools of learning; knows comparatively nothing of philosophy, systematic or historical theology; and is totally ignorant of the dead languages." The case came to trial March 17, 1913, in the Police Court of Hamilton. During five hours of cross-examination the Pastor admitted he had attended school for only seven years. Then Ross's attorney turned to the question of languages.

ATTY. STAUNTON: Do you know the Greek alphabet?
RUSSELL: Oh, yes.
STAUNTON: Can you tell me the correct letters if you see them?
RUSSELL: Some of them. I might make a mistake on some of them.
STAUNTON: Would you tell me the names of those on top of the page, page 447 I have got here?
RUSSELL: Well, I don't know that I would be able to.
STAUNTON: You can't tell what those letters are? Look at them and see if you know.
RUSSELL: My way . . . (the judge interrupted at this point)
STAUNTON: Are you familiar with the Greek language?
RUSSELL: No.

The attorney went on to get admissions from Pastor Russell that he knew no more Latin and Hebrew than he did Greek. The Pastor lost the case.

Actually what the Pastor had become quite adept at was matching the words in a lexicon with a word-for-word translation of the Bible. Perhaps he applied more logic to his system than the art of linguistics allows, since he insisted that one Greek or Hebrew word must have but one meaning. Naturally he and his successors produced interpretations strikingly original in comparison with the efforts of scholars concerned with context and nuances of expression.

A second favorite method of the Pastor was to string Biblical passages together to prove his points. Professor Bruce M. Metzger of the Princeton Theological Seminary elaborates: "By thus joining together portions of Scripture which were never intended to go together it is possible, of course, to prove anything from the Bible. The method, if it can be called a method, is seen to be reduced to an absurdity if one should quote in succession the following three passages of Scripture: 'Judas went out and hanged himself' (Matt. 27:5); 'Go, and do thou likewise' (Luke 10:37); 'What thou doest, do quickly' (John 13:27)! To be specific, the bizarre eschatological teaching of the sect is due quite largely to an arbitrary combining of certain Biblical passages mingled with many a gratuitous assertion." [17]

Until 1908 the Society operated out of Pittsburgh but the expanding publishing and organizational activities made the need for more room imperative. The Pastor evidently thought it might also be wise to leave the vicinity of his marital difficulties. He bought a four-story brownstone in Brooklyn which had been the parsonage of Henry Ward Beecher, minister of Plymouth Congregational Church. In order to hold property in New York he formed another corporation which he labeled the People's Pulpit Association. He purchased a nearby mission church known as Plymouth Bethel. The old Beecher mansion was rechristened Bethel and the church was renamed the Brooklyn Tabernacle, with seats for 800.

The Pastor started a newspaper syndicate in 1910 and telegraphed his weekly sermons to subscribing papers. This work reached its peak in 1913 when more than 1,500 newspapers were printing his words, but was abandoned in 1915.

The Pastor arranged for an annual pilgrimage to London and added preaching and inspection trips to the Continent. Sales of his books reached the millions and subscriptions to the *Watch Tower* mounted.

Anticipating the later movie spectaculars, the Pastor devised an ingenious *Photo-Drama of Creation.* Using slides, motion pictures and phonograph records he produced a remarkably advanced audio-visual aid in a primitive New York studio. The project cost the Society more than $300,000. Work began in 1912 and continued through the early months of 1914. The complete show consisted of two four-hour parts with a synchronized narration. The Society prepared a number of sets and eventually as many as 35,000 people a day were watching this program. The total number of people who saw the *Photo-Drama* has been estimated at 9,000,000.

The climax approached. The unheeding world celebrated New Year's Eve on December 31, 1913, and entered the fateful 1914 when the Pastor had calculated that the nations would finally be overthrown and the new creation of Jehovah God set up in their place.

The Pastor had taught that the number of human beings who would ever reach heaven was fixed by the Bible at 144,000. Most of these heaven-destined people had already died but a remnant remained on earth.

Old-time Russellites waited expectantly for what some had been preparing for since the early 1880's. As members of the remnant of the 144,000, they thought they would soon join Jesus in the spirit life. Recent converts thanked God they had heard the message of salvation in time's nick. But as the weeks and months of 1914 rolled by, the Pastor nervously began to hedge his predictions. He cautioned patience and warned against those who presumed to set a specific date for the end. And by the end of the year of decision (December 15) he was writing: "Even if the time of our change should not come within ten years, what more should we ask? Are we not a blessed, happy people? Is not our God faithful? If anyone knows anything better, let him take it. If any of you ever find anything better, we hope you will tell us."

Charles Taze Russell joined the long roster of prophets of doom who lived to see their doomsday come and go. Of course, new interpretations were advanced. The Society did not disintegrate on December 31, 1914. Years later Russell's successor as president of the Watchtower Society would reveal what really had taken place in 1914. This year was the start of a tremendous battle in heaven between Satan and Jesus. Jesus had won and cast Satan down to the vicinity of the earth. Since the devil now had to confine his evil-doing to our planet, he stirred up the World War, the famines, the breakdown of morals in the postwar years, and the other ills that plague us.

In ailing health Pastor Russell embarked on a barnstorming preaching tour in the fall of 1916. He stopped off at Detroit and Chicago, Houston and San Antonio. His last public lecture was delivered in Los Angeles on October 29, 1916. He had to sit down during his talk. He told his traveling companion Menta Sturgeon he would cancel the rest of his tour and head for home.

His Atcheson, Topeka and Sante Fe train stopped at a siding in dusty Pampa, Texas. The dying Pastor made a final request of his companion: "Make me a Roman toga." Brother Sturgeon did the best he could with some Pullman sheets. He called the conductor and the porter and said, "We want you to see how a great man of God can die." The bearded, sixty-four-year-old patriarch gathered the sheet around him, drew up his feet on the bed like Jacob of old, and passed away.

He might have become one of the nation's business tycoons but he turned to the study of the Bible and left an estate of only $300. Lacking any high-school much less college education and any ability in scriptural languages, he was able to convince tens of thousands that his interpretations of the Bible showed most of the central Christian beliefs to be in error.

He apparently believed himself to be the "faithful and wise servant" mentioned in Matthew 24:45-47. The *Watchtower* would later declare that he was "undoubtedly this same angel," as in Ezek. 9:1-11. This was the "seventh messenger of the Church" who "filled the office foreshadowed by the Prophet Ezekiel as represented in the man clothed in linen with a writer's inkhorn at his side."

Judge Rutherford would say, "His explanatory writings on the Bible are far more extensive than the combined writings of St. Paul, St. John, Arius, Waldo, Wycliffe, and Martin Luther—the Six Messengers to the church who preceded him." A few weeks after his death the Judge declared, "He did a greater work for the cause of the Messiah's Kingdom than did any other man that ever lived on the earth." [18]

Yet in a few years his books could be found only in second-hand stores and by 1951 the cult he founded would ask: ". . . who is preaching the teaching of Pastor Russell? Certainly not Jehovah's Witnesses! They cannot be accused of following him, for they neither quote him as an authority nor publish nor distribute his writings." [19] Modern Witnesses seem to have washed their hands of the Seventh Messenger.

A critic of the movement, Charles W. Ferguson, wrote in 1929:

> Inherently, he was no more regal and heroic than, say, Calvin Coolidge. He had his virtues, to be sure, but in everything he did there was something just the least bit pathetic. Earth clung to him relentlessly. He was never admired by those who hated him. To read intimate accounts of his daily life is to suffer with the hero in a realistic novel; he was piteous and depressing.[20]

His Great Pyramid fancies, 1914 prophecies, and marital troubles would only embarrass today's eager Witness of Jehovah. He would be like a slobbering and eccentric grandparent at an organization man's cocktail party. His books and tracts—some 50,000 pages in all—would require too many explanatory footnotes and editings. He would have much to learn from Brothers Rutherford and Knorr before he could join in a Kingdom Hall discussion. He had simply thought there was something wrong with hell-fire and had prowled through the Scriptures to see if he could discover what thousands of orthodox theologians through the ages had missed. He thought he had.

3. *Judge Rutherford: "Millions Now Living Will Never Die"*

PASTOR RUSSELL's death on the Pullman car in Texas left the Bible Students shaken and confused. Some imagined they would soon follow the Pastor into the Kingdom and others thought the missionary or harvest work completed. The *Watchtower* explains:

> Though they had expected that with the establishment of Jehovah's kingdom by Christ their work on earth would be finished and they would be taken to heaven, they began to learn that there was other work entrusted to them.[1]

Annual election of Watchtower officers was two months away. In the interim an executive committee took over. During his lifetime Russell encountered no opposition and was routinely re-elected president of the various corporations. Every contributor to the cause received one vote for each $10 and of the total of 150,000 votes the pastor himself held 25,000. These died with him. (In 1944 the election machinery would be changed to provide for one member, one vote.)

One man, the Society's legal adviser, seemed the natural successor to the colorful and controversial Pastor. One of the few professional men to join the movement, Joseph F. Rutherford (born November 8, 1869) became a full-time Pilgrim in 1907, a year after his baptism.

He grew up on a farm in Missouri in a Baptist family distinguished for its austerity and strict discipline. His father objected to the idea of higher education but finally consented to allow his son to attend an academy if he would hire a substitute to take over his own farm chores. According to the official history of the Watchtower Society, Rutherford completed his formal education, spent two years as a legal apprentice and had become a court reporter by the time he reached the age of twenty.

At twenty-two, young Rutherford was admitted to the Missouri bar and began to practice law in Booneville. He later served four years as public prosecutor. On several occasions Rutherford took his turn as stand-in when the regular judge fell ill. On the basis of this service (about four days in all) he became known as "the Judge" although he was never elected or appointed to a judgeship. He never referred to himself by this title but his followers and publicity men regularly called him Judge Rutherford.

Two ladies called on him in his law office in 1894 and persuaded him to buy three books by Pastor Russell, but he delayed joining the cult for a dozen years. He met Pastor Russell around the turn of the century and the Pastor urged him to express his religious views in print. The result was a book entitled *Man's Salvation from a Lawyer's Viewpoint.* He received baptism in 1906 and soon took over the legal work for the Pastor; by this time he was a mature man with almost 20 years of legal experience behind him.

Few real judges looked more like a judge than Rutherford. Tall (6 feet, 4 inches) and dour, he usually appeared in a wing collar and black bow tie with a cane or umbrella on his arm. A dark ribbon around his neck held his reading glasses.

The cult's official history goes so far as to call him "brusque and direct" [2] and comments on his "unusual directness in dealing with associates." [3] This brusqueness and directness contrasted strikingly with the personality of the easygoing, gregarious Pastor Russell. Nevertheless Rutherford won the top spot with a unanimous vote and set about to remake the Watchtower in his own image and likeness.

One of his first targets was "creature worship"—which was euphemistic for lingering adulation of the departed Russell. Many devotees considered Russell to be the "wise and faithful servant" mentioned in Matthew 24:45. During his lifetime the sly old Pastor neither confirmed nor denied this interpretation. Rutherford would make it plain that this "servant" referred to a group of people (the Watchtower Society) rather than to any single individual.

Soon after taking office Rutherford boosted the number of full-time Pilgrim missionaries and attempted to involve the entire congregation in door-to-door witnessing, an assignment formerly reserved for the ladies only. He devised a quiz for male members and authorized those who scored 85 per cent or higher to accept public-speaking engagements on Bible topics.

Trouble first came in the person of one P. S. L. Johnson. Born a Jew, converted to Christianity and ordained a Lutheran minister, Johnson had finally seen the light of Russellism. He had been sent to supervise the work of the Society in England. Apparently he overplayed his hand and tried to take over the Society in that country. Rutherford cabled him to return to Brooklyn and give an account of his stewardship. Chastened and disgruntled, he persuaded four of the seven members of the board of directors to combine against the newly elected president.

Publication of the seventh volume of Russell's *Studies in the Scriptures* triggered the open revolt against Rutherford's administration. The Judge had secretly commissioned two Bible Students to compile Russell's biblical commentaries on Revelation and Ezekiel into a posthumous volume. Unknown to the dissidents on the board, the Judge shepherded the book through the press and announced its publication at the dinner table at Bethel Home on July 18, 1917. Furious at not being consulted, the rebels agreed to present their case against Rutherford at the forthcoming Boston convention. Local congregations were torn between Rutherford and the rebels.

The canny Judge, however, served as permanent chairman of the Boston meeting and, as the official historians admit, "in this way he was able to control every session, and those in opposition were not permitted at any time to address the assembly." [4] This muzzling further frustrated the protesting board members who had organized a Committee of Seven.

Rutherford now drew on two decades of experience as a small-town lawyer and sprang a legal maneuver which stripped the dissenters of any authority within the Society. Russell had been accustomed to fill the positions of deceased directors by personal appointment; technically these appointments had to be reconfirmed by vote. Nobody had dared to suggest to the Pastor that he adhere to the constitution and he had never bothered to submit his appointments to the formality of a vote. Rutherford discovered that the rebel board members had all been appointed by Russell but never confirmed by vote. The Judge now declared them to be usurpers. He and his two colleagues on the board held their posts legally since they had been elected officers of the board. The four dissenters were ousted and replaced by Rutherford men.

About 4,000 rebels left the Society to form splinter sects, leaving 17,000 faithful to the new Rutherford regime. Johnson soon got into an argument with the other four and went his own way. Some of these offshoots persist to this day and are discussed in Chapter 13.

Distribution of the disputed seventh volume, which was called *The Finished Mystery,* brought further trouble to the battle-scarred sect. During the first week of publication the Society sold 32,000 copies at 60 cents a copy. By October 850,-000 copies had been sold and it had been translated into several languages. The book launched an all-out attack on organized religion; it lumped Catholics and Protestants together as forming a "modern-day Babylon." Marley Cole, apologist for the cult, describes the book as a "spiritual deathblow to Christendom." In particular *The Finished Mystery* singled out Christian clergymen as hypocrites, tools of Satan, and unworthy shepherds.

Largely because of this book the government of Canada banned the Society on February 12, 1918. Judge Rutherford attributed this action to the machinations of priests and ministers. Wide-swinging attacks on such a basic social institution as the church by a cult which resisted military service brought the Watchtower to the attention of the wartime U. S. government. Rumors popped up that German officials had visited Brooklyn Bethel just before the United States entered the war. Army intelligence and secret service agents raided Watchtower offices on both coasts in search of incriminating correspondence or publications. Finally on May 7, 1918, the federal government issued a warrant for the arrest of eight Watchtower officials on charges of sedition.

Specifically, Rutherford and his seven associates were charged with violating the Espionage law by obstructing recruitment and enlistment in the armed forces and with encouraging insubordination. The trial lasted 15 days and the verdict was guilty on four counts. Judge H. B. Howe fumed: "If they had taken guns and swords and joined the German army the harm they could have done would have been insignificant compared with the result of their propaganda."

Seven of the defendants received 20 years on each of the four counts to run concurrently and the eighth received a ten-year sentence. After the verdict was announced the Bible Students in the courtroom broke into the old hymn "Bless'd Be the Tie That Binds." The defendants marched out of the courtroom with pink carnations in their lapels. Judge Rutherford told a newspaper reporter: "This is the happiest day of my life." He added: "To serve earthly punishment for the sake of one's religious belief is one of the greatest privileges a man could have." He blamed the Christian clergy and the instigators of the recent schism for his predicament.

Considering the temper of the times, no other verdict seemed likely. Other Bible Students were being dragged through the streets of American cities for refusing to buy Liberty bonds or trying to escape military service. Attempts to sell copies of *The Finished Mystery* invited a jail term or tarring and feathering. Not more than 4,000 hard-core followers stayed with the Society as the nation crusaded against the Kaiser.

In Atlanta penitentiary Rutherford first worked in the tailor shop but was later transferred to the more congenial atmosphere of the prison library. The eight men organized Bible classes among the inmates and the Judge composed a weekly epistle to his followers on the outside. Nevertheless the imprisonment of the top officials threw the tiny sect into a panic and thoroughly disrupted its activities. Practically all evangelistic work ground to a stop. The cult sold its Brooklyn Tabernacle, closed Bethel Home and moved back to an office building in Pittsburgh. But delegates to the next convention showed their loyalty to the Judge by re-electing him president despite his confinement in the federal prison.

Stalwarts circulated petitions to release the eight from their "Babylonish captivity." More than 700,000 signatures were collected in March 1919. After nine months in prison the Watchtower officials were released on $10,000 bail pending trial. Before the end of the year the court would declare: "The defendants in this case did not have the temperate and impartial trial to which they were entitled, and for that reason the judgment is reversed." The federal government finally withdrew prosecution and later Rutherford appeared before the Supreme Court of the United States, which would have been forbidden if he were held to be an ex-convict.

That the imprisonment of the sect's leaders was a miscarriage of justice would be hard to deny. Only the hysteria of World War I and the understandable reaction of some Christians against the outrageous libeling of their clergy can explain this episode. The Judge's prison experienec helped shape his later conception of a separate nation for Jehovah's people—the Theocracy—and no doubt hardened his attitude toward both civil authorities and the clergy.

With its leaders free again, the cult began the work of rebuilding. The Brooklyn Tabernacle had been sold, the residents of Bethel were dispersed. Printing plates had been destroyed and the cult no longer owned any presses of its own. Immediately after his release from Atlanta, Rutherford took off for California to visit his family and try to regain his health. He had contracted a lung disorder in his damp prison cell which plagued him until his death.

Even through the bleak days of the Atlanta confinement the remaining Bible Students managed to get out regular issues of the *Watchtower*. At the first post-Atlanta reunion assembly in 1919 Rutherford revealed plans for a companion journal to be called the *Golden Age*. Its contents were less theological and esoteric than the *Watchtower* and was frankly designed for the nonbeliever more than the Russellites. The cult moved back to Brooklyn in 1919.

By the time of the 1922 convention at Cedar Point, Ohio, the missionary character of the rejuvenated movement was evident. Three thousand Bible Students gathered to hear the Judge urge them to "Advertise, Advertise, Advertise the King and the Kingdom!"

Meanwhile the Judge began a sweeping doctrinal reform. The official history concedes: "There were many false doctrines and practices that had not yet been cleaned out of the organization." [5] Among these was an emphasis on character development, creature worship (of Charles Taze Russell), the celebration of Christmas, the use of the cross as a Christian symbol, failure to give due honor to the proper name of God (Jehovah), and a democratic congregational-type of church government. These errors were said to have been "inherited from the pagan traditions adopted by Christendom."

Apparently Rutherford did not recognize these errors at this stage of the Society's history or at least did not do anything about them. In 1929 he was still using the cross to illustrate his books; little attention to the use of "Jehovah" as referring to the deity can be seen before 1931; and "theocratic" polity did not replace congregationalism until 1938.

Rutherford's special political target during these postwar years was the new League of Nations. This he branded a confederation of Satan's principalities, as his successors would later brand the United Nations. The general endorsement of the Geneva organization by the Federal Council of Churches of Christ did little to endear the League to the Judge's heart and only confirmed his low estimate of organized Christianity.

As late as 1923, in a pamphlet entitled *World Distress, Why? The Remedy,* the Judge was still making use of Pastor Russell's Great Pyramid calculations to buttress his Bible chronology. Rutherford eventually jettisoned the Great Pyramid Theory and insisted that only the Bible itself was a trustworthy guide to prophecy. Pagan pyramids were no longer to be looked to as clues to the future. He also gave up the use of the many elaborate charts which had fascinated Russell and which he sprinkled through his scriptural commentaries.

Only once did the Judge try his hand at date setting. In 1920 he predicted that the princes of the Old Testament—Abraham, Isaac, Jacob *et al.*—would be resurrected in 1925. They would come back to life just before the opening guns of Armageddon. When 1925 saw no sign of these personages, the Judge quietly dropped the matter although he purchased a mansion for their use in California and lived in it himself from 1930 to 1942.

To a newspaper reporter the Judge explained, "I purposely landscaped the place with palms and olive trees so King David and these princes of the universe will feel at home when they come to offer man the chance to become perfect."

By the end of the 1920's the memory of the Pastor was dim except in the hearts of old-timers and close friends. Most Bible Students by this time had never known the Pastor personally, since the schisms, Atlanta imprisonment and defections had left only a handful of pre-1916 Russellites in the Watchtower organization.

Early in his term as president, the Judge had visited London, Glasgow, Egypt and Palestine to meet foreign Bible Students and to add personal experiences in the Holy Land to his Bible sermons. The Society acquired modern printing equipment to publish the *Watchtower,* the *Golden Age,* and tracts. In a basic policy change the Pilgrims and volunteer door-to-door salesmen were instructed to sell rather than to loan Watchtower literature. Rutherford's first full-length book, the *Harp of God,* sold for 68 cents postpaid and was the first break from the exclusive use of Russell's seven volumes. Later Rutherford titles included *Deliverance* (1926), *Creation* (1927), *Reconciliation* (1928) and *Government* (1928). Press runs regularly topped one million copies, which enabled the cult to offer a hard-bound book of several hundred pages for a fraction of the cost of secular best sellers.

During the 1920's billboards and barn posters, sandwich men and newspaper ads repeated the Judge's favorite slogan: *Millions Now Living Will Never Die.* By this he meant that mankind was now in its latter days and that a favored few who accepted the Watchtower message would live through the coming battle of Armageddon.

In speeches and books Rutherford castigated what he termed an evil triumvirate of organized religion, politics and big business. He called the Christian clergy the victims of "spiritual leprosy." Lay Christians who opposed or ignored the Watchtower were described as "lovers of self, covetous, boasters, unthankful, unholy, fierce, despisers of those who strive to be good, heady, high-minded, having a form of godliness but denying the power thereof, and who slander, misrepresent and persecute those who faithfully try to represent our Lord."[6] The Judge's followers marched in front of Catholic churches during Sunday Mass with signs proclaiming RELIGION IS A SNARE AND A RACKET and expressed amazement that the worshipers took offense.

Thirty thousand people packed the Los Angeles Coliseum in 1923 to hear the Judge blast the "God-dishonoring doctrines of higher criticism and evolution." To this day the Witnesses carry on a running battle against the evolutionists, maintaining that mankind was created approximately 6,000 years ago. In Indianapolis the Society's convention approved a resolution that charged that "the religionists, both Catholic and Protestant, are conspicuous by their arrogance, self-conceit, impiety and ungodliness."

In 1925 the Judge revealed that as a result of a war in heaven commencing in 1914, Satan was cast down and has been confined to the vicinity of the earth. This vindicated Pastor Russell's prophecies regarding the mystical significance of 1914 and also explained the rash of wars, natural disasters, financial shenanigans and loose living of the Roaring Twenties. Judge Rutherford also assured the Bible Students that they would not actually take part in Armageddon but were charged with warning men of good will to escape with them and observe the carnage and defeat of Satan from the sidelines.

Membership sagged in 1925 and a number of recent converts turned away from the Society. Slightly more than 89,000 participated in the Lord's Evening Meal in the spring of 1926, which was fewer than the year before and reversed the pattern of growth which began after the 1919 reorganization. To win additional converts the cult inaugurated Sunday morning canvassing of householders in 1927.

Quick to adopt new evangelistic methods, the Society set up its own radio station, WBBR, on Staten Island. It beamed Watchtower programs to New York City, Connecticut and New Jersey. At one time or another the Society also operated six smaller stations around the country, including WORD in Batavia, Illinois. Rutherford recorded a series of short sermons which were furnished to a "wax network" of several hundred cooperating stations.

Bethel Home supplied most of the manpower for the cult's headquarters in Brooklyn. The 1928 *Yearbook* reported that 180 people, mostly young men, lived in Bethel. Living facilities in Brooklyn had been enlarged. The original Beecher brownstone together with two adjacent buildings had been razed in 1926 to make way for a 9-story residence and office building.

The Judge settled a long-standing problem in 1931 when he told a convention in Columbus, Ohio, that he had decided on "Jehovah's witnesses" as the proper name for the brethren. He got the inspiration from Isa. 43:12—"Ye are my witnesses, saith the Lord." Changing "the Lord" to "Jehovah," he came up with Jehovah's witnesses, which the Society always spells with a small *w*. Before this they had been known as Bible Students, Millennial Dawnists, Russellites, Watchtower people, Rutherfordites, etc. The new name emphasized the growing significance of the proper name of God in the doctrines of the cult. It also supplied an aura of antiquity, since all references to "witnesses" in the Old or New Testament could be interpreted to mean "Jehovah's witnesses," their spiritual ancestors. The first Witness was said to be Abel.

From his Brooklyn headquarters the contentious Judge hurled challenges to debate theological issues with leading fundamentalist preachers and even with Pope Pius XI, who did not reply. Most of his invective against organized religion was reserved for the Roman Catholic Church and its hierarchy. Cartoons in Watchtower tracts depicted fat, scowling priests and nuns as powers behind the thrones of Nazism and fascism.

Fifty policemen guarded the Witnesses meeting in two Plainfield, New Jersey, theatres while the Judge delivered his typical anti-Catholic harangue. A line of Witnesses six miles long paraded through downtown Newark carrying signs damning religion. These tactics brought quick retaliation and soon the Witnesses were standing trial for selling books without a license, disturbing the peace, inciting to riot, and so on. The cult's legal department kept busy advising hundreds of arrested Witnesses and supplying lawyers. Witnesses staged mock trials serving as defendants, judges and prosecutors. Watchtower attorneys briefed the brethren on how to act when arrested, how to reach a lawyer, how to stand trial.

At the first indication of trouble in a community a Witness was told to phone Brooklyn to initiate countermeasures. Through call committees the cult could assemble caravans of from 10 to 200 automobiles. Meeting at a predesignated rendezvous the drivers would descend on the community. With such blitzkrieg methods the Witnesses were able to sweep through the town with door-to-door calls in one or two hours. "This arrangement made it possible to overwhelm the opposers by sheer numbers so that, no matter how 'hot' the territory was, practically every house was reached with the good news of the Kingdom." [7] Sometimes a few would be arrested but the town jails soon filled up and the rest would usually be allowed to continue their calls unmolested.

Rutherford's vicious attacks on religion and the clergy did cost him his radio outlets. Catholics and Protestants deluged local station managers with protests and petitions against the Watchtower transcriptions until most stations capitulated. The Society's counterpetitions to the FCC got nowhere. Reduced to a handful of holdout stations, the Judge decided to withdraw from the air in 1937. From then on the Society limited its broadcasting to its own stations. It bought a fleet of sound trucks to carry its message to rural communities but it never re-entered the radio field nor has it ever gone in for television on any large scale.

Early in the doorstep campaigns the Witnesses were encouraged to memorize one-page sermonettes. Now to make up for the loss of the radio work and to guarantee uniform doctrinal expositions, the Society turned to the portable phonograph which was soon to become its trademark. Furnished at cost to members, the phonographs enabled tongue-tied Witnesses to bring the voice of the Judge into thousands of homes every Sunday morning. Rutherford recorded 83 separate 4½-minute talks.

The Judge tossed a doctrinal bomb into the 1935 convention in Washington, D.C. Russell had taught that an additional class of men besides the anointed 144,000 would share a spirit life in heaven with Jesus Christ. They would not rank as high as the 144,000 but neither would theirs be an earthly destiny. Now Rutherford produced scriptural evidence to disprove the existence of any such secondary spiritual class. He explained that all men would reach one of three ultimate destinations: spirit life in heaven as one of the select 144,000, everlasting life on a paradisical earth, or annihilation.

Until the middle of the 1930's the chief aim of the cult's missionary efforts had been to identify and gather the remnant of the 144,000. Since this quota had been filling up since the first Pentecost, relatively few candidates remained on earth. Russell could presume that all his followers belonged to the remnant, but the growth of the Society called for some explanation by Rutherford. Obviously even many who joined Jehovah's Witnesses could not claim a place among the 144,000. Their task was now defined as assisting the remnant in establishing the Theocracy and extending the message about Armageddon to millions of "other sheep" who could live through the battle into the New World.

Meanwhile overseas the Society faced serious difficulties. The large German Society aroused the ire of the new Nazi government when Witnesses refused to salute the swastika or serve in the army. The Judge and the Watchtower business manager, Nathan H. Knorr, made a quick trip to Germany in 1933 to persuade the Nazis to return Watchtower property. They did temporarily restore the property, held in the name of an American corporation, but clamped on restrictions which severely curtailed Witness activities.

Italy banned the Society in 1932 and Japan followed suit in 1939. At the start of World War II the Nazis repossessed all Watchtower property and converted it to government use. In protest, congregations of Jehovah's Witnesses in 50 countries wired identical telegrams to Chancellor Hitler as follows: HITLER GOVERNMENT, BERLIN, GERMANY. YOUR ILL TREATMENT OF JEHOVAH'S WITNESSES SHOCKS ALL GOOD PEOPLE OF EARTH AND DISHONORS GOD'S NAME. REFRAIN FROM FURTHER PERSECUTING JEHOVAH'S WITNESSES; OTHERWISE GOD WILL DE-

STROY YOU AND YOUR NATIONAL PARTY. Hitler did not listen.

Christian Front followers of Father Coughlin tried to break up a Witness rally in Madison Square Garden in 1939. About 500 Frontists and German-American Bundists started to yell and toss vegetables during Rutherford's address to 18,000 faithful. Cane-swinging Witness ushers cleared the balconies and during the scuffle which followed, three Witnesses were arrested for felonious assault. A court of three judges—two Roman Catholics and a Jew—commended them for their restraint and ordered them released.

In London the underground Irish Republican Army issued bomb threats but Witness meetings continued and the threats never materialized. English judges seldom granted draft exemptions to Witnesses; Canada and Australia banned all Witness activity early in the war.

Gradually the Judge developed his ideas of a separate theocracy of Jehovah's Witnesses which began in his Atlanta cell. From a tiny band of unorthodox Bible students under Pastor Russell the cult moved to a position of proletarian estrangement from secular society. Witnesses no longer took an active interest in the affairs of Satan's world. They refused to render military service, vote, hold public office, buy government bonds, salute the flag. They withdrew from most secular contacts such as active union membership, PTAs, social clubs, lodges. With Armageddon so near they pooh-poohed the idea of a college education for their children, who could better spend the time warning others to flee from the wrath of Jehovah. For a period, the cult actively discouraged marriage itself. Rutherford's book *Children* released in 1941 relates the story of two young Witnesses who decide to wait until after Armageddon to get married.

Russell had introduced the same church policy he had

known as a young man: congregationalism. For many decades each ecclesia of Bible Students elected its own elders and reported their names to Brooklyn. Rutherford set out to tighten control of the Society and in 1932 he managed to get the elders replaced by a service committee. Finally in 1938 the cult announced a complete change from congregational to "theocratic" control. From then on, local officers got their appointments from Brooklyn and not from their congregations.

Mob action against the unpopular Witnesses grew as the nation edged toward war. During the question-and-answer period at the 1935 convention the Judge had declared that it was unfaithfulness to Jehovah to salute any earthly emblem. The litigation involving members of the sect who refused to salute the flag, to register for military service, and to abide by local ordinances restricting their missionary work is summarized in Chapter 11.

Witnesses thwarted what they called an American Legion-inspired raid on their farm in South Lansing, New York, on Flag Day, June 14, 1940. Hundreds of automobiles converged on the farm but a tipster warned the Witnesses, who summoned state police and deputy sheriffs. The officers refused to allow anyone to leave his car and thereby broke up the plan of attack. Witnesses estimated there were 1,000 cars in the area with perhaps 4,000 hostile Legionnaires involved.

In the midst of these troubles Rutherford issued a call for another national convention. Witnesses usually welcomed the announcement of a convention since this meant that Armageddon was not too close at hand. Considering the sentiment of the nation at this time, some Witnesses may have restrained their enthusiasm for this particular assembly.

The Judge contracted for use of the state fairgrounds at

Columbus, Ohio, but Governor Bricker canceled the contract and refused to reconsider his decision. Instead the Witnesses switched their meeting to Detroit where 35,000 men, women and children met in makeshift quarters. To maintain order and dissuade hecklers, official Witness bouncers carried heavy canes and the Judge reportedly stationed several guards on the rooftop because he expected Catholic priests to try to bomb the site from an airplane. After all, Father Coughlin himself presided over a parish in nearby Royal Oak; but the controversial radio priest probably had neither a pilot's license nor inclination to bomb the conclave. The now-ailing Witness patriarch appeared three times before cheering Witnesses.

Another technique was added to the Witnesses' missionary apparatus. Until 1940 the Witnesses concentrated on calling on householders on Sunday morning or offering tracts and booklets to worshipers leaving church. Now the cult equipped volunteers with magazine bags and assigned them to peddle copies of *Watchtower* and *Consolation* (the new name for the *Golden Age*) for a nickel on street corners.

In his later years Judge Rutherford avoided close contact with his followers and became almost a legendary character. He was known to the average Witness as only a somber voice on a phonograph disk. He never much enjoyed meeting people or preaching to crowds as did the Pastor. The Judge ducked all news photographers and declined to submit a write-up for *Who's Who in America.*

After the Detroit assembly he retired to the Witness-owned mansion in San Diego, California, which he had occupied on and off since 1930. The Judge had predicted that a group of Old Testament princes would lend their administrative skills to the organization of the New World Society. The San Diego estate, known as Beth Sarim, or "House of Princes," would serve as their home and headquarters. The deed was therefore made out to Abel, Noah, Abraham, David, etc. In the meantime the Judge set up housekeeping on the premises.

Except for one intramural incident the Society was untroubled by schisms or dissension in the Judge's declining years. In 1939 the Judge's successor as legal adviser was ousted from the corporation. Olin R. Moyle had dared to criticize certain aspects of the Society which the faithful had now come to regard as divine in nature. Specifically Moyle objected to the Judge's abusive public scoldings at the Bethel dinner table, what he termed the Judge's high style of living at Bethel and Beth Sarim, and the use of liquor and vulgar language at Bethel. When the Judge turned his verbal artillery on the unfrocked Moyle the latter entered suit against Rutherford and the other board members for libel. He won the suit in 1944 and collected $25,000.

By this time the verdict did not matter to the Judge. After directing the Society for 25 years and two days Judge J. F. Rutherford died of cancer at Beth Sarim on January 8, 1942. He was seventy-two. He had averaged a full-length book a year and during his last year on earth he had seen more than 36,000,000 copies of his books and pamphlets distributed in dozens of languages. Few men have ever been able to reach so many by means of the printed word. He had seen the Witnesses grow from a dispirited, loosely organized band to a self-confident theocratic society of 106,000.

Cantankerous, aloof, legalistic and vindictive, Rutherford tolerated no disloyalty or criticism within the cult. He engendered fear and respect more than the affection which the Bible Students held for Pastor Russell. He knew how to employ the talents of his subordinates wisely: Knorr handled the business affairs and printing operation; Hayden Covington became one of the top constitutional lawyers in the country; Fred W. Franz concentrated on Biblical and doctrinal elaboration.

In his final instructions the Judge directed that he be buried at dawn on the day after his death. He specified the spot —a hillside crypt at Beth Sarim; but his wishes could not be carried out since the county forbade burial outside of certain zones. His body was interred five months later in Rossville, New York.

In a sense, his role in the Witnesses paralleled that of Brigham Young in Mormonism. Answering inquirers as he pushed West, Young had only one explanation for the Mormon exodus: "To get away from the United States and the Christians." The frontier was gone. Judge Rutherford nevertheless led his followers into the wilderness of the Theocracy. They became strangers in the lands of their birth, men without a country, Philip Nolans.

In a few years the San Diego mansion was sold. The Judge's books were allowed to go out of print even as he allowed Russell's books to disappear. His wife and only child, Malcolm, never participated actively in the movement and some doubt exists that they ever accepted the cult's teachings.

To modern converts Judge Rutherford, like Pastor Russell, has become merely a shadowy figure in the history of Jehovah's Witnesses. And there were those who wondered why of the millions now living who would never die, the Judge was not counted among them.

4. *President Knorr Remodels the Watchtower*

AT PASTOR RUSSELL'S DEATH, control of the Watchtower Society passed from a self-taught theologian-preacher to a small-town lawyer. At Judge Rutherford's death in 1942 control passed to an organization man who had spent most of his adult life working in the business end of the Society at Brooklyn headquarters.

The man elected to the lifetime post of president of the three corporations was only thirty-six at the time. Born on April 23, 1905, in Bethlehem, Pennsylvania, Nathan Homer Knorr completed his formal education on graduating from the Allentown high school in 1923. He and his family had been attracted to the doctrines of the Watchtower while he was a sophomore. This led to his withdrawal from the Reformed Church.

Young Knorr became a full-time pioneer the year he got his diploma and went to the Brooklyn headquarters to work in the shipping department of the printing plant. While living at Bethel Home he also traveled within a 200-mile radius of Brooklyn giving weekend Bible lectures. His unusual business ability came to the attention of the Society's hierarchy and he was asked to take on the task of coordinating all the printing activities. At twenty-seven Knorr became general manager of the publishing operation and the office.

His climb up the Society's ladder of authority began with his election in 1934 as a director of the People's Pulpit Association (now called the Watchtower Bible and Tract Society of New York). A year later he was elected vice-president of this corporation and five years after this he became a director and vice-president of the original Pennsylvania corporation as well. As an officer of these two corporations Knorr acknowledged that he believed himself to be one of the 144,000 anointed who would one day reign with Christ in heaven.

Knorr devised the basic zone system in which each zone would include 20 congregations under the direction of a zone servant. He persuaded the Judge to adopt the reorganization in 1938. In his first year as president Knorr would again reorganize the zones into circuits. He would also direct each circuit to sponsor two assemblies a year.

Members of the New York and Pennsylvania corporations met in the parlors of Bethel on the afternoon of January 13, 1942—only a week after the Judge's death—and elected Nathan Knorr president. His takeover encountered none of the opposition and rebellion which faced Rutherford in 1917.

Knorr applied all his energy and organizational abilities to the task of expanding and perfecting the Society. The year he assumed command the *Yearbook* reported 115,240 Jehovah's Witnesses throughout the world; within 20 years the third president could report a 700 per cent increase.

The quarter century of Judge Rutherford's rule had left

its imprint on the tiny band of Jehovah's Witnesses. They had won a reputation for orneriness. Their one-foot-in-the-door tactics, dourness, and belligerent attitude toward householders and passers-by who failed to heed their warnings of Armageddon earned them an understandable opprobrium in many communities.

Knorr, the salesman, realized that these tactics had to be modified. Nobody sells his product whether Fuller brushes or the New World Society by insulting potential customers, playing a recorded sales talk, or reciting a prepared statement. The young president mapped out a thorough public relations face lifting which has accounted in large measure for the impressive membership gains since 1942.

He first junked the phonographs and recordings of Judge Rutherford's sermonettes. He realized that regardless of their educational limitations his Witnesses could not convince others by simply parroting the Judge's words or playing a phonograph on the doorstep. They would accomplish far more if they stood on their own two feet and delivered a short face-to-face homily. Their hosts would forgive a few grammatical lapses. But the Witnesses could not gain the needed confidence and fluency without preparation.

Knorr prescribed a massive adult education program in the form of a weekly theocratic ministry school designed to turn Witnesses, especially the men, into assured, friendly, Bible-saturated salesmen for the new religion. Bashful Witnesses were forced to work up short talks and submit them to congregational criticism at the weekly sessions. Over the weeks and months, garage mechanics and factory workers and farmers developed into rather polished speakers.

Another public relations tool was revealed in 1945 when Knorr directed all local congregations to sponsor regular public meetings. Witnesses distributed handbills on Main Street on Saturday inviting their neighbors to attend the one-hour program in Kingdom Hall the next afternoon. To ensure uniformity of presentation the Society distributed one-page outlines for a series of eight public talks. The Witnesses also emphasized that no collection plate was passed.

To discourage the growth of any cult of personality Knorr decreed that in the future all publications of the Society would be published anonymously. No one but the top officers of the Society knows exactly who writes the books, magazine articles and tracts which flow from Brooklyn's presses. Even correspondence from the Society is simply rubber-stamped WATCHTOWER BIBLE AND TRACT SOCIETY. The only by-lines in the *Watchtower* are given to pioneers and Bethel residents who recount their conversions and happiness at being Jehovah's Witnesses.

Early in his presidency Knorr visited branches in Mexico, the Caribbean, Central and South America. He recognized the great potential for growth in these traditionally Roman Catholic areas. The lingering Christian faith, scarcity of Catholic priests and sisters, and latent anticlericalism provided a good seedbed for the New World Society.

In the past, overseas expansion in mission territory had been more or less haphazard. Many nations, especially in Asia and Africa, reported no Witnesses at all. Despite the difficulties of communication and travel in the middle of World War II, Knorr set the Society on a course leading to a systematic missionary effort.

He founded the Watchtower Bible School of Gilead at South Lansing, New York, to train full-time missionaries who would go wherever they were sent to establish Witness enclaves. The first graduating classes headed for Latin America and after the war Gilead graduates were sent to Asia, Africa and Europe as well. Without these dedicated men and women from the Gilead short course we probably would not have seen the world-wide expansion of the Society during the past two decades.

Wartime bans did not seem to slow Watchtower growth. By the end of the war the *Yearbook* reported three times as many publishers as in 1939. Banned in Canada for three years during the war, the Society nevertheless managed to grow from 6,000 to 10,000 publishers.

A Jesuit scholar, the Rev. Neil G. McCluskey, describes some of the features of the Knorr remodeling: "The vicious and lurid literature of the Rutherford era began to be quietly toned down. A certain smattering of biblical and historical scholarship began to perfume the newer tracts and books. Most of Rutherford's violent polemics, meaning the bulk of his writings, along with his own redoubtable person, were by degrees assigned to the same limbo of oblivion to which he had consigned the movement's founder, Charles Taze Russell." [1]

President Knorr commissioned a band of veteran Witnesses, some of them college graduates, to try their hand at a new translation of the Bible. Cults often express their impatience with the "faulty" translations in current use. His action was reminiscent of the attempt of Joseph Smith, Jr., author of the Book of Mormon and founder of the Mormon church, to provide a new translation of the Bible for his followers. Today the Reorganized Church of Jesus Christ of Latter-day Saints of Independence, Missouri, still uses this "Inspired" translation but the main Utah branch never adopted it.

The Watchtower translation committee released the New

World Translation of the Christian Greek Scriptures in 1950. The first of five volumes of the New World Translation of the Hebrew Scriptures appeared in 1953 and the last in 1960. The Society objects to the terms New and Old Testaments.

Naturally the translators took the opportunity to confirm certain Witness beliefs and emphases. They inserted what they considered to be the proper name of God—Jehovah—where the traditional versions use Lord or God. They changed cross to torture stake and tried to clarify certain passages relating to *sheol* (hell) and the immortality of the soul. The New World translation of the Lord's Prayer reads as follows:

> Our Father in the heavens, let your name be sanctified. Let your kingdom come. Let your will come to pass, as in heaven, also upon earth. Give us today our bread for this day; and forgive us our debts, as we also have forgiven our debtors. And do not bring us into temptation, but deliver us from the wicked one.

Of course, the translators knew that the Hebrews refused to write or speak the divine name of God but used instead an abbreviation called the Tetragrammaton. The Jews substituted the word "Adonai" (Lord) for the Tetragrammaton: JHVH.

Eventually some Christians decided to take the vowels from "Adonai" and insert them between the consonants in JHVH, changing the initial vowel to *e* for easier pronunciation. They came up with "Jehovah." Nobody knows for sure how the divine name was pronounced in ancient times but almost everyone, including the Watchtower translators, agrees that it was probably closer to "Yahweh" than "Jehovah." Logically then with their insistence on the importance of the proper name of God, the Witnesses should be known as "Yahweh's Witnesses." The translation committee explains:

> While inclining to view the pronunciation "Yah-weh" as the more correct way, we have retained the form "Jehovah" because of people's familiarity with it since the 14th century. Moreover, it preserves, equally with other forms, the four letters of the Tetragrammaton JHVH.[2]

The outsider might be tempted to ask why they attach such importance to the traditional way of pronouncing the Tetragrammaton while excoriating those orthodox Christians who revere the cross rather than the torture stake. Certainly the people's familiarity with the cross as the instrument of Jesus' death goes back much farther than even the fourteenth century.

The New World translations do not include the so-called Apocrypha in the Hebrew Scriptures. These books—Tobit, Judith, Wisdom of Solomon, Ecclesiasticus, Baruch, 1 and 2 Maccabees, a supplement to Esther and three additions to Daniel—are accepted by Roman Catholics as deuterocanonical. Luther gathered the eleven writings and put them between the Old and New Testaments. They were included in the King James version and the tendency in modern translations has been to include these writings.

For years the Society had favored a Bible called the "Emphatic Diaglott" prepared by Benjamin Wilson, a Geneva, Illinois, newspaper editor who was not a Russellite. The Society acquired a set of New Testament plates in 1902 and later printed a Bible on its own printing presses. Eventually they received permission to use plates of the American Standard Version, to which they attached an Appendix.

When the first New World volume was introduced in 1950 Knorr explained:

> We do not discourage the use of any of these Bible versions, but shall ourselves go on making suitable use of them. However, during all our years of using these versions down to the latest of them, we have found them defective. In one or another vital respect they are inconsistent or unsatisfactory, infected with religious traditions or worldly philosophy and hence not in harmony with the sacred truths which Jehovah God has restored to his devoted people who call upon his name and seek to serve him with one accord.

The New World committee went back to the original Greek text of the New Testament, using that of Westcott and Hort. They modernized archaic vocabularies but stuck to a literal translation. One of their basic principles would appeal to the amateur linguist but horrify the professional: they determined to attach one meaning to every word regardless of context. Unfortunately, as their critics soon pointed out, language is often not that logical. Members of the translation committee were to remain anonymous even after their deaths.

Orthodox clergymen admired the ambition of the cult to undertake such a job with the brainpower available to them but they could not accept the Society's translation as a significant contribution to biblical knowledge. Professor H. H. Rowley of the University of Manchester wrote a scathing review in *The Expository Times.* He entitled his review "How Not to Translate the Bible." Professor Bruce M. Metzger reviewed the first volume in the *Princeton Seminary Bulletin* for Spring, 1951. He wrote:

> The decision to render, so far as practicable, the same Greek word by the same English word has a specious show of faithful-

ness to the original, but the application of the principle with any degree of consistency tends to a certain woodenness and actual impoverishment of the original. Here the guiding maxim of that wise and veteran translator, St. Jerome, is eminently sound; he resolved, he says, to translate not words but the sense.[3]

Professor Rowley is even harder on the Witness scholars:

They profess to offer a rendering into modern English which is as faithful as possible. In fact, the jargon which they use is often scarcely English at all, and it reminds one of nothing so much as a schoolboy's first painful beginnings in translating Latin into English. The translation is marked by a wooden literalism which will only exasperate any intelligent reader—if such it finds—and instead of showing the reverence for the Bible which the translators profess, it is an insult to the Word of God.[4]

He concludes his review:

From beginning to end this volume is a shining example of how the Bible should not be translated, and a reminder that the Bible is great literature, which deserves to be translated by those who have a feeling for style and who both understand the original and know how to express its meaning with elegance.[5]

Most dedicated Witnesses now own a set of these approved volumes for use in their private Bible study and Kingdom Hall classes but continue to refer to the King James, Revised Standard or Catholic versions in their door-to-door ministry. Catholics and Protestants might understandably express some suspicion if doctrinal points were fortified by recourse to a special translation by the cult's anonymous scripture scholars.

Rutherford considered hymn singing a waste of time but

Knorr reintroduced singing and music to Kingdom Hall meetings and assemblies. The Society now issues a songbook called *Songs to Jehovah's Praise*. Among the 88 hymns are:

Forward! You Witnesses
Theocracy's Increase
I am Jehovah!
Joyous Theocratic Activity
Forward! Theocratic Warriors!
The Taunt-Song Against Satan

Today Witness platform lecturers do not hesitate to insert an anecdote or joke in their presentations which the stern Judge would certainly have branded as frivolous. Much of the blatant anticlericalism and anti-Catholicism has been curtailed. At least Witnesses do not stake out churches on Sunday mornings to display RELIGION IS A RACKET banners as they once did. The caricatures of bloated monsignors and beak-nosed ministers no longer enliven *Watchtower* and *Awake!* pages.

Knorr again employed the screen as a propaganda device even as Pastor Russell's *Photo-Drama* had served the early movement. A 90-minute film entitled *The New World Society in Action* was released in 1954. The first half of the film depicted activities of the Society including scenes at Brooklyn headquarters; the second half was filmed in color at the 1953 international assembly and a district assembly in Africa. Following the 1958 assembly in New York City the Society distributed a full-length film in color which was widely shown at public meetings and circuit assemblies.

President Knorr continued the policy of encouraging all Witnesses to defend and protect their civil rights. He backed the Society's policy of carrying all adverse decisions to higher courts. This part of the Society's history will be discussed in Chapter 11.

Knorr saw the public relations value of the huge assembly. He called together the first international assembly in New York City in 1950 which drew a peak attendance of 123,000, including 10,000 from other countries. The 1953 convention was even larger and the 1958 one holds the record as their largest religious gathering, with more than 253,000 at the final Yankee Stadium-Polo Grounds session.

Physical expansion was crowned by completion of a 13-story addition to the printing plant in 1957. In 1950 the Society spent a substantial amount of money improving the broadcasting facilities at WBBR on Staten Island. They boosted its power from 1,000 to 5,000 watts but in 1957 the Society sold the entire station, explaining that it no longer served the interests of the Kingdom. Perhaps television stole its listening audience.

Knorr travels about 50,000 miles a year and has visited more than 85 countries. He is a non-smoker who takes an occasional glass of wine and avidly follows the fortunes of the New York Yankees. He married Miss Audrey Mock, a co-worker and resident at Bethel, in 1953. Easily accessible to Bethel workers, Knorr holds an informal court after every meal in the refectory to hear problems and receive suggestions. He routinely refuses to grant any interviews and the Society publishes only a pedestrian one-page biographical sketch. His lectures are the features of international and regional assemblies and he is a good speaker.

Second in importance in the Watchtower hierarchy is a sixty-eight-year-old native of Kentucky and graduate of the University of Cincinnati, Fred W. Franz. He serves as Knorr's theological adviser and traveling companion since he knows

Spanish, Portuguese, German and a smattering of French. Franz entered the work on a full-time basis in 1914 and was hand-picked by Rutherford to be his editorial assistant. He serves as vice-president of the two American corporations while Grant Suiter holds the post of secretary-treasurer. Considering Franz's age, Suiter would be the more logical choice to succeed to the throne in the event of Knorr's death.

The grand old man of the movement is octogenarian A. H. Macmillan, who was baptized in 1900 and knew both Russell and Rutherford intimately. He is known and loved by Jehovah's Witnesses around the world and has become a familiar figure at assemblies. Macmillan authored a book about his life, conversion and impressions of the Society, one of the rare literary efforts by a Watchtower insider to be published by a secular publisher. It came out in 1957 with a cautious "imprimatur" by Knorr. Some of his younger colleagues would no doubt have preferred that he had kept some of his observations, especially those on the Judge's personality defects, to himself.

The work of Jehovah's Witnesses is carried out through three legal corporations. The original corporation founded in 1884 by Russell in Pittsburgh was called Zion's Watch Tower Tract Society. Its staff moved to Brooklyn in 1909 although a small office is still maintained in Pittsburgh. Meanwhile in 1896 Russell had changed the name to the Watch Tower Bible & Tract Society.

In 1909 the Pastor organized the People's Pulpit Association of New York, U.S.A., which was later changed to the Watchtower Bible & Tract Society, Inc., some thirty years afterward. This corporation owns the property used by the older Pennsylvania corporation. In theory the New York corporation directs the activities in the United States while the

Pennsylvania corporation handles operations in foreign countries. To arrange for ownership of property in certain foreign nations a third corporation was formed in London in 1914: the International Bible Students Association. Knorr heads all three legal bodies for life.

At one time the faithful who contributed $10 to the Pennsylvania corporation were counted as members of the corporation. They received an additional vote for each extra $10 donation. In 1944 the financial contribution requirement was dropped and membership on the board was limited to 500, with no fewer than 300. A recent survey of the board members indicates that two out of three claim to belong to the remnant. Their average age is nearly sixty and most board members have been associated with the work for 25 years or more.

The New York corporation is a self-perpetuating body of 400 Witnesses who elect a seven-member board of directors. All offices are held for life. Information on the identity of board members or election procedures is not available to the ordinary Witness or investigator. At any rate, President Knorr holds absolute power and the various corporation directors and board members serve as no check or balance.

During Nathan Knorr's 20 years as president the Society has gained in members, resources, geographical distribution and respectability. Should he remain in office for another 20 years he may find himself at the head of a major religious denomination. Of course, he confidently expects Armageddon to begin before that.

5. *The Theology of Jehovah's Witnesses*

If we were asked to give a capsule description of the Witnesses of Jehovah as theologians we might call them fundamentalist unitarians. They regard the Bible as the infallible word of God, a word which must be taken literally and at face value. At the same time they stoutly deny the divinity of Jesus Christ and the doctrine of the Trinity.

They differ from Protestants and Catholics in also rejecting the idea of the immortality of the human soul, the existence of hell or purgatory, the value of the sacraments and the visible Second Coming.

An orthodox Christian theologian would recognize bits and scraps of a dozen ancient heresies in contemporary Witness theology. He would see traces of Gnosticism, Manichaeanism and Docetism in Russell's system, but most of all he would see a revival of Arianism. Arius (280–336 A.D.) was a priest in Alexandria who denied the divinity of Jesus and regarded him as simply a superior creature or angel sent by God to save the world. He and his followers, especially Eusebius of Nicomedia, threatened to overwhelm the orthodox body in number and influence but were condemned by the Council of Nicea in 325. Athanasius led the anti-Arian party.

Like other chiliastic sects, the Watchtower Society likes to rummage around in the apocalyptic books of Daniel and Revelation. They claim to base all their doctrines on the Bible alone and believe that no one else reads the Scriptures with the same open mind they do. The "nominal" Christians of Christendom bring along a bagful of pagan notions, papal errors, the prejudices of the Church Fathers, modern scientific theories such as evolution and higher criticism to their study of the Bible and therefore they miss the true meaning.

The Witnesses refuse to accept the idea of "mystery" in the Bible. They seek to apply the rule of reason to all doctrines. Pastor Russell attacked the Trinity from strictly rational grounds: "At the same time it is admitted that the doctrine [of the Trinity] is incomprehensible, and therefore that nobody really believes it, because nobody can in a true sense believe an incomprehensible thing." [1] The orthodox Christian will be more likely to admit his inability fully to understand such problems as the existence of evil and suffering, predestination, and the Trinity of Three Persons in One God. But the Witness ridicules the idea of a "three-headed" God while finding no difficulty in accepting as literally true the story of Jonah and the whale, the intermarriage of angels and men to produce monsters known as Nephilim, and the minute details of the Genesis account of creation.

In a burst of candor Judge Rutherford even disclosed that Jehovah resides in the constellation Pleiades. This information appeared in his book *Reconciliation* (1928), p. 12. This seems to be the only reference to Jehovah's home in *Watchtower* literature.

Jehovah's Witnesses worship a God of vengeance, justice

and law who seems to fit into the Old Testament context better than the New. He is a God who plans the utter destruction of the present religious, political and commercial classes.

The Seventh-day Adventists, theological cousins of the Witnesses, report that God is particularly angry with men because they observe Sunday as the Lord's Day instead of the Jewish Sabbath, Saturday. The Witnesses tell us what really arouses the wrath of God is the failure of Christians to use his proper name, Jehovah. Instead, nominal Christians call Him Lord or God. In their New World Translation of the Bible the Witnesses have restored the name Jehovah more than 6,000 times where the other translations use substitute names.

Jehovah is not three but one, say the Witnesses. The Holy Ghost is not a person in a trinity but merely a term signifying the power of Jehovah. He whom orthodox Christians call the Second Person of the Trinity, Jesus Christ, is rather the first of Jehovah's spirit sons. Another name by which he has been known is Michael the Archangel. Satan invented the doctrine of the Trinity to seduce men into accepting false religion. Russell explains: "Nimrod married his mother, Semiramis, so that in a sense he was his own father, and his own son. Here was the origin of the Trinity doctrine." [2]

Jehovah used his first created son, Michael (or Jesus), as a working partner in creating the world. "Christ Jesus, also called Logos, was the first creation of God, and was thereafter used as a Master Workman in successive creative works," writes Knorr.[3]

Another spirit son was given the job of overseeing the creation of the earth but he grew jealous when he saw the worship and honor given to Jehovah God by the earth creatures. This was Lucifer, who ranked next to Michael in Jehovah's favor. In his rebellion he became known as Satan and as Satan he has carried out a constant and cunning warfare with Jehovah. He claims as his allies organized religion, worldly governments, business and commerce, and most of mankind. Although they deny the existence of hell, the Witnesses pay more attention to Satan and his activities than any major Christian denomination.

Adam and Eve were created by Jehovah, placed in the Garden of Eden, and given the opportunity to live forever on this earth glorifying their Creator and filling the earth with their offspring. The first pair was created approximately 6,000 years ago. They spoke Hebrew and lived in an area we know called Armenia. "The speech with which He endowed Adam and Eve in Eden was Hebrew." [4]

Satan in the guise of a snake tempted Eve to eat of the fruit of the tree of knowledge and she in turn tempted Adam and caused him to disobey Jehovah's command. Both sinned and were turned out of paradise. Through this disobedience Adam lost his original perfection, as did all his descendants. Jehovah declared that man like the dog and the worm would die and cease to exist altogether. The Witnesses insist that man does not *have* a soul but he *is* a soul. They reject any suggestion of a dual body and soul nature. "The first man, Adam, was created a living soul, and nowhere is it stated that he was given an immortal soul." [5]

Basic Witness doctrine declares: "Immortality is a reward for faithfulness. It does not come automatically to a human at birth." [6] The doctrine of immortality is branded as the "foundation doctrine of false religion." [7]

Adam lived to be nine hundred and thirty years old. Cain, Adam's first son, murdered Abel, who is considered the first

Witness of Jehovah. Things went from bad to worse after the murder of Abel. Disobedient angels had sexual intercourse with human females and gave birth to freaks and giants known as Nephilim. Finally in disgust Jehovah decided to wipe out all mankind except for the upright Noah and his family. The Witnesses pinpoint the date of the flood in the year 2370 B.C.

Everyone on earth was killed by the flood except the passengers on Noah's ark and the wicked angels who returned to spirit bodies. Jehovah entered a covenant with mankind: "If any human soul ate blood, killed animals without cause or murdered another man, he would be breaking the rainbow covenant. . . . Since this eternal covenant is binding upon all mankind, no one is free to disobey it." [8] This is the chief reason why the Witnesses now oppose blood transfusions, since they interpret eating blood to mean either by mouth or by veins.

Just as Adam sinned and Cain slew Abel and the people grew wicked, so Noah's descendants forgot about Jehovah and righteousness. "It was from the city of Babylon that false religion was carried to all parts of the earth. Because of the bad influence of this false religion the worship of almost all people today is not pleasing to God. Their religions are to him like the smell of rotting flesh in a hot sun." [9]

Abraham, the father of the chosen people of Israel, was born 352 years after the flood. Eventually Moses led the chosen people out of Egyptian bondage and wrote the Book of Genesis. The Witnesses explain that Adam knew how to write and set down what Jehovah had told him about creation. He used clay tablets which were copied by others and finally reached Moses himself.[10]

After Adam's sin Jehovah had promised to ransom mankind

from the punishment of death. Since Adam was a perfect man when he fell from grace, only another perfect man could deliver the ransom to Jehovah. The ransom had to be no more and no less than the life of another perfect man. The death of a god would be too much and the death of an imperfect descendant of Adam would be too little. To accomplish this redemption and lift the penalty of death, Jehovah's first-begotten spirit son agreed to assume human form as a perfect man and to give his life as the ransom. Jesus (Michael) left heaven and became a perfect man—"absolutely sinless, guileless, undefiled."

Jesus was born of a virgin in Bethlehem on October 1, 2 B.C. He grew up in Egypt and Nazareth with four brothers and an undetermined number of sisters. At the age of thirty he was anointed and became the Messiah. He then spent three and a half years in his teaching mission, performed miracles, chose 12 apostles and a number of disciples, and finally was impaled on a torture stake by his "religious enemies" on April 1, 33 A.D.

> On the third day of his being dead in the grave his immortal Father Jehovah God raised him from the dead, not as a human Son, but as a mighty immortal spirit Son, with all power in heaven and earth under the Most High God . . . For forty days after he materialized, as angels before him had done, to show himself alive to his disciples as witnesses.[11]

Judge Rutherford speculated:

> The bodies in which Jesus appeared after his resurrection were neither the body that was crucified nor his glorious spiritual body, but bodies created expressly for the purpose of appearing unto his disciples. Our Lord's human body, the one

crucified, was removed from the tomb, by the power of God... We can only surmise that the Lord may have preserved it somewhere to exhibit to the people in the Millennial Age.[12]

The Witnesses say that Jesus died on the stake to show that a perfect man could obey Jehovah God despite the temptations of Satan, to show that a mighty spirit creature such as he would be obedient to Jehovah although Lucifer was not, and finally to remove the penalty of death from mankind. Today Jesus serves as Jehovah's executive officer as ruler of the Theocracy in heaven and on earth.

Although Jesus founded a church, pagan error infiltrated into its pure doctrine. Of course, the Witnesses reject the Roman Catholic interpretation of Matthew 16:18 in which Christ tells Peter that he is a Rock and upon this Rock He would build His church. Like most Protestants, the Witnesses maintain that Jesus meant that He would build His church on Himself as the Great Rock. They deny that Peter held any place of primacy among the apostles.

If Lucifer, Adam and Israel could fall away from Jehovah so could the Christian Church, reason the Witnesses. Soon Christians were believing in the immortality of the soul, the Trinity, an eternal hell and other "pagan" doctrines. The Protestant Reformation did little to remedy the situation or strip away these "pagan" accretions. "While called the Reformation, his [Luther's] work was more a rebellion against the pope than a reformation by a full return to the Bible." [13]

From the day of Adam's fall until 1914 A.D., Satan ruled the earth. Through the power of Jehovah a few men and women began to restudy the Bible in the 1870's. They were headed by Pastor Russell. But the Witnesses indignantly deny that their movement was founded by the Pastor:

True, since the nineteenth century men such as C. T. Russell and J. F. Rutherford took a prominent part in this world-wide work as Jehovah's witnesses, even as in ancient days Christ Jesus, Paul, Peter, John the Baptist, Moses, Abraham, Noah, Abel and many others participated prominently in the work of Jehovah's witnesses. Yet it is Scripturally and factually clear that only Almighty God Jehovah himself founded or ordained and continues to ordain his witnesses, and in proof of this he gives them his name.[14]

Through the ages a few men here and there remained true to Jehovah amidst the general apostacy of the Christian Church. But it was not until the formal organization of the Watchtower Society that Jehovah blessed the body of believers.

Pastor Russell decided that the Second Coming was an invisible rather than a visible event and it had taken place in 1874. For 40 years Jehovah collected his flock on earth and in 1914 Jesus engaged Satan in a great heavenly war which lasted 1,260 days. Jesus won and Satan was thrown out of heaven to the vicinity of this planet. Satan must now confine and concentrate his mischief-making to our planet-home. Pastor Russell, however, did not know about this battle in the heavens, since it was not revealed to the faithful until much later by his successor, Judge Rutherford.

Although contemporary Witnesses disagree, the facts seem clear that the pastor and his followers fully expected 1914 to bring about the dramatic and final end of things in this old world. When nothing of this nature happened, except the start of World War I, many of his followers slipped away and the Pastor himself confessed his puzzlement at the miscalculation. The current Watchtower explanations are of post-Russell vintage.

Men have often speculated about the end of the world, the last things, and it is in this area of eschatology that the Witnesses have spun their most elaborate doctrinal theories. Before the final establishment of Jehovah's theocracy this world must undergo the harrowing battle between the forces of good and evil called Armageddon. "After almost six thousand years of human sorrow, suffering and death, at last permanent relief is near at hand and will be realized within this generation." [15] This relief, the righting of all wrongs and injustices and the comeuppance of all the wicked, will come through the victory of Jehovah at Armageddon. The battle might begin next week, tomorrow, before you finish reading this page.

The Witnesses do not predict a definite year or day for the start of the battle. What they do emphasize is that Armageddon will certainly begin during the lifetime of some people who were alive in 1914. "We know Armageddon is near for another reason. Jesus said that the generation of people living when the 'time of the end' began would not pass away before Armageddon breaks out. . . . Many are the people alive since 1914 who will still be living when it is time for Armageddon to begin." [16] Exactly how long is a generation? The Watchtower prophets do not specify but conversations with many Witnesses indicate that they all expect Armageddon before 1972.

On the side of righteousness at Armageddon will be Jehovah, the Supreme Commander, and His son, Jesus, His field marshal. On the opposing side of the battle line will be arrayed all the forces of evil and privilege: Satan and his demons, religionists, the apathetic, persecutors of Jehovah's Witnesses, political and commercial bigwigs. Witnesses who live to see the battle commence will not be called upon to participate as combatants themselves but will observe the action from a safe distance. Jehovah, of course, will defeat Satan and his allies.

Armageddon will start with an avalanche of natural disasters: earthquakes, plagues, cloudbursts and floods, gigantic hailstones, a rain of fire. Most of mankind, terrified as they might well be, will try to flee to the mountains and from the hands of their fellow men. Those who escape being murdered by their fellows will be slain by Christ's avenging angels.

The earth will be littered with millions upon millions of dead bodies. For seven months the survivors of Armageddon will go about burying the rotting flesh and bones. "Armageddon is over. Gone now are the invisible troublemakers! Gone are all the nations! Gone are all the goatlike people! Gone is the old world—gone forever. A new world begins." [17]

For another seven years the survivors will clean up the ruins and begin to construct the homes and parks of the new paradise on earth. The work progresses under the direction of "princes" such as Abraham, Moses and David of the pre-Christian era together with certain of the "other sheep."

Most Christian churches promise the reward of heaven to those who believe in Jesus Christ, are baptized and lead a good life. The Witnesses believe and teach that only a tiny fraction of mankind will ever get to heaven. The Bible, they insist, has set the number of those destined for heaven at 144,000; they refer to various passages in Revelation as proof. The first of these 144,000 were the 120 men and women chosen at the first Pentecost; these 144,000 constitute a group known variously as the spiritual class, anointed, the bride of Christ, the little flock, spiritual Israelites.

Only these few thousands of the billions of men and women who have inhabited this globe will pass into a spirit existence after death and assist Jesus as "associate Kings" in governing creation. Most of the 144,000 have already died and gone to heaven but a remnant of about 13,000 still live in our midst. They all happen to be Jehovah's Witnesses.

Judge Rutherford disclosed in 1927 that the spiritual Israelites who had died prior to 1918 were raised to life in heaven in that year. Members of the remnant who have died since then do not spend any time in the grave but are immediately taken to heaven.

Most of Jehovah's Witnesses belong to another class not destined to attain heaven. These are the "other sheep" or "Jonadabs." Faithful Witnesses of Jehovah will survive the holocaust of Armageddon—"millions now living will never die"—and their reward will be life everlasting on a purified earth. Their number, unlike that of the anointed, is unlimited and especially since 1931 the Watchtower Society has been bringing its message to these other sheep. Before that the main effort of the Society was to discover and enroll the living members of the 144,000. The duty of the "other sheep" is to assist the remnant in reaching still other "other sheep" and warning them to flee to the safety of the ark of the New World Society if they wish to escape imminent destruction. Only by serving the remnant, preaching the message, and submitting to a dedicatory baptism can men and women hope to live through the great battle.

Armageddon's human survivors will never die, get sick, want for material things. They will never get to heaven but will live forever in a reconstructed Garden of Eden as mankind was supposed to do before Adam sinned. To the oppressed and disinherited masses, the Society paints a glowing picture of the simple joys and happiness of the post-Armageddon theocracy. In the New World there will be no police or soldiers, no famines, no sickness, no bad weather, no insect pests, no water shortages, no wild animals, no cheating, no crime. The survivors will even continue to marry and beget children until the earth is comfortably filled with the survivors, their families, and the men and women resurrected from the memorial tombs.

For the Armageddon survivors and their offspring will not be the only inhabitants of the New World. They will be joined by the resurrected people who were Jehovah's Witnesses during life or who never had an opportunity to hear the gospel. The irreformable wicked will neither be resurrected nor will they be punished in either a temporary purgatory or an eternal hell. They will simply be annihilated. Their memory will be lost to the minds of men and Jehovah. "Those who die wicked beyond reform or correction and beyond redemption by Christ's blood will not be brought out of the grave to judgment in the New World." [18]

First to be resurrected from the dead will be Abel and the Old Testament prophets who will become "princes" of the New World. Then will come forth Witnesses of Jehovah who happened to die before Armageddon. Finally Jehovah will bring back the "unrighteous" who did not hear the Watchtower message or whose lives were not thoroughly wicked. An example of someone in this class will be the good thief who was executed next to Christ and to whom Christ promised paradise. These "unrighteous" will be given a fair chance to hear and accept the truth but if they remain unconverted or unwilling to throw in their lot with the New World they will suffer the same fate as the deliberately wicked: annihilation.

A *New Yorker* writer worries about the post-Armageddon population explosion:

Even if, as the Witnesses believe, mankind is only 6,000 years old, well over 250 billion people have lived on the earth, by one estimate, and the lists of the fallen but reformable will have to be culled pretty rigorously if the Witnesses themselves are going to have enough room to turn around in, let alone do any repopulating of the Globe.[19]

Witnesses categorically deny the existence of hell. They consider the doctrine of an eternal hell to be unscriptural, unreasonable, contrary to God's love and repugnant to justice.

Who is responsible for this God-defaming doctrine of a hell of torment? The promulgator of it is Satan himself. His purpose in introducing it has been to frighten the people away from studying the Bible and to make them hate God. Imperfect man does not torture even a mad dog, but kills it. And yet the clergyman attributes to God, who is love, the wicked crime of torturing human creatures merely because they had the misfortune to be born sinners. (I John 4:16) The hell-fire doctrine was taught by pagans hundreds of years before Christ. It, as well as the doctrine of "purgatory," is based on another pagan false doctrine, that of the immortality of the human soul. To suffer eternal torment in consciousness after death the human soul would have to be immortal and indestructible.[20]

Whatever terms are used in the Bible, say Witness theologians—*sheol,* Gehenna or hades—they all refer simply to the state of the dead. Since all surviving men will either go to heaven or enjoy an eternal paradise on earth, the Witnesses may be called not only unitarians but universalists. If everyone will not be saved, neither will anyone suffer eternal punishment.

Eventually, then, all men will end up in one of three categories. If a man belongs to the select 144,000 he will enter a spirit life in heaven with Jesus. If he is a faithful Witness of

Jehovah or a fairly good man who accepts the Theocracy after his resurrection, he will live forever in a paradise on this earth. Finally, if he is wicked in this life or stubbornly set against his conversion in the next, he will be annihilated, completely destroyed, forgotten.

(Until the 1935 convention in Washington, D. C. the Society taught that a fourth class of people would appear before Armageddon who would also enjoy spirit life but on a lower plane than the 144,000. They were said to be the "great multitude" mentioned in Revelation 7:9. Judge Rutherford, however, announced that this class was one and the same as the "other sheep" who would live on this planet forever. That settled the matter and no more has been heard about this fourth category.)

After 1,000 years of this idyllic existence on a renewed earth Jehovah will once again release Satan from the abyss to test the faith of mankind. Some men and women will succumb to the temptations of the great seducer and both they and the devil will finally be annihilated. The rest will go on living on earth forever. Eventually Armageddon's survivors will stop having children so that everyone will have some space in which to move around.

The duty of Jehovah's Witnesses today, whether of the elite remnant or the other sheep, is to warn as many people as possible of the battle which begins at any moment. Other things can wait—praying, giving alms, setting up schools, staffing hospitals, caring for the aged and orphaned. The sole task is to reach as many people of good will as they can so that they too can find shelter in the New World Society. Unconverted, they may never experience the resurrection after the battle or may lack the faith to withstand Satan's final assault at the end of his 1,000-year captivity.

The religion of Jehovah's Witnesses is activist or it is nothing. The salvation of the ordinary Witness consists in obeying the directions of the remnant expressed through the Watchtower Society. He must study the Bible, Watchtower books and magazines. He must warn his neighbors about Armageddon and make a careful count of the hours spent in such activity as well as in Bible study, back calls, and so on.

If a convert wishes to become a full-fledged Witness of Jehovah he must finally repent of his sins and undergo baptism by immersion. Baptism is not a sacrament; it does not wash away sins, but for those who are alive at the start of Armageddon it does lift the penalty of death.

Before going into the water the candidates for baptism are asked to give their answers to two questions:

"Have you recognized yourself before Jehovah God as a sinner who needs salvation, and have you acknowledged to Him that this salvation proceeds from Him, the Father, through His Son, Jesus Christ?"

"On the basis of this faith in God and in His provision for salvation, have you dedicated yourself unreservedly to God to do His will henceforth as He reveals it to you through Jesus Christ and through the Bible under the enlightening power of His Holy Spirit?"

All shout "Yes."

Since the theology and organization of the Society depend to such an extent on the distinction between the remnant and the other sheep, we may ask how an individual knows to which class he belongs. The modern Witness faces somewhat the same problem as the Calvinist who was concerned to know if he belonged to the elect or the damned. One test the Calvinist employed was that of prosperity. If the Calvinist prospered in his business affairs he concluded that his election was fairly certain, since surely God would favor those whom He had chosen. Such a dollars-and-cents test would hardly suit the Witnesses.

Most Witnesses simply conclude that they do not belong to the remnant. To qualify for the remnant a Witness would have to testify to a special conviction of his membership in the 144,000 and a strong longing for a heavenly destiny. The average Witness cheerfully admits he will be quite happy to spend eternity right here on earth. He does not wish to leave his family, parents and friends and his own physical body to spend an eternity in spirit form. The Watchtower board of directors and officers and many Bethel Home residents, full-time overseas missionaries, and circuit servants consider themselves among the 144,000. The Society expects the number of the remnant—now about 13,000—to decrease each year and discourages the garden-variety Witness from getting any ideas that he has been so chosen by Jehovah.

During Russell's era and the early part of Rutherford's regime, practically everyone who attended the Memorial Supper received communion since they all believed themselves to be part of the remnant. In 1938 there were 69,345 people in attendance and of these 36,732 partook, a percentage of 52 per cent. By 1961 this had dropped to less than 1 per cent of those attending the service.

To uphold their view of special creation the Witnesses take on both the scientists and fundamentalists. They scorn the fundamentalist view that the days of creation were 24-hour days. A "day" really means 7,000 years, say the Witnesses. This means that the start of the week of creation was in the year 46,026 B.C. The six days of creation as outlined in Genesis do not include the period of perhaps billions of years

Judge J. F. Rutherford headed the Watchtower Society for 25 years. He composed the slogan "Millions Now Living Will Never Die" and coined the name Jehovah's Witnesses in 1931.

Wide World Photos

Judge Rutherford died at Beth Sarim, a mansion owned by Jehovah's Witnesses in San Diego, California, in 1942. The $75,000 residence was purchased in 1930 to serve as headquarters for the resurrected Old Testament "Princes."

United Press International

More than 600 men and women live at Bethel Home in Brooklyn, New York. All residents receive room, board and $14 a month as a living allowance.

The Watchtower Society operates one of the largest, most modern printing plants in the country. This plant in Brooklyn turns out more than 125,000,000 books, magazines and tracts a year. All employees—linotypists, pressmen, proofreaders, binders—live at Bethel Home, a few blocks away.

Wide World Photos

A huge tent-and-trailer city housed 30,000 Witnesses attending the 1953 assembly in New York City. The site was 25 miles from the city in Piscataway, New Jersey.

More than 252,000 people jammed Yankee Stadium *(below)* and the Polo Grounds for the final session of the 1958 assembly in New York City. This was the largest convention the nation's largest city had ever entertained.

Nathan H. Knorr has headed the Witnesses of Jehovah since 1942 and has seen membership increase 800 per cent since then. He joined the Witnesses during high school and assumed the top position at the age of thirty-six.

Mystery writer Mickey Spillane conducts a home Bible class shortly after his conversion to Jehovah's Witnesses in 1952. U. S. Witnesses sponsored 194,000 such classes during 1960.

United Press Internat

The average Witness puts in about ten hours a month in door-to-door preaching or street-corner sales of Watchtower publications. The total number of hours reported by Witnesses in such activities around the world in 1960 exceeded 131,000,000.

Baptism by immersion symbolizes member's dedication to Jehovah. Baptized Witnesses are considered full-fledged ministers, not merely members.

Witnesses held the largest mass baptism in history at Orchard Beach in the Bronx during the 1958 assembly. A total of 7,136 men, women and children were immersed on July 30.

United Press International

in which the earth was a formless waste. This spares them embarrassment when geologists produce evidence of rocks and fossils millions of years old.

The scientist cannot help the Witnesses out when it comes to the age of man. The Witness theologians insist that Adam and Eve appeared on the scene in the year 4025 B.C. On the other hand, the most conservative scientist would estimate that man has been on earth for at least 600,000 years.

Holding the position that man does not have a soul but is a soul, the Witness cannot reconcile the theory of evolution and religion as can the orthodox Protestant or Catholic. The latter can admit that man's body may well have evolved from lower life, and this over a period of millions of years, while insisting only that at some point God infused a soul which distinguishes men from other animals.

That orthodox religion has generally managed to survive the skepticism of Darwin's theories and has made an accommodation with modern science only confirms the Witness in his opinion of Christendom:

> When religious compromisers say evolution might have been used by God in creating, they ignore his expressed law that his creations bring forth offspring "after their kind." The evolutionary doctrine can no more be proved from scientific fact than orthodox religion's teachings can be proved from the Bible. Dazzled and flattered by the wisdom of men, both modern science and false religion are blind to the wisdom of God, blind to the truths of his Word, blind to the most vital knowledge of these days, that Bible chronology and signs of the times herald the incoming of a glorious new world of righteousness.[21]

The same pamphlet concludes:

> Study the Bible, so that you can show your love for the

Creator by serving him. Its truth will free you from the pagan myth of evolution. Heed God's advice: "Shut your mind against these profane, drivelling myths." (I Timothy 4:7, *Moffatt;* I Thessalonians 5:21.) When the divine showdown between this drivelling myth and the new world comes, soon, it will be as though a bubble got in the path of the earth. Satan's evolution will never survive its collision with Jehovah God's new world.[22]

Besides the basic difference between the Witnesses and orthodox Christians in believing Jesus to be an angel-turned-perfect-man instead of the Second Divine Person of the Trinity, the Witnesses hold a number of other positions at variance with the mainstream of Christian thought. For example, they refuse to celebrate Christmas since they claim to know that the real date of Jesus' birthday is October 1, 2 B.C. They say the December 25 date is of pagan origin and that the Bible nowhere tells Christians to observe birthdays, their own or anyone else's.

Like many Protestants, they uphold the Virgin Birth but deny the Catholic doctrine of the Immaculate Conception. They also deny the perpetual virginity of Mary. Her role in the plan of redemption is minimized. "Mary was conceived in sin and born in error." [23]

Unlike the Holiness sects in the fundamentalist tradition, the Witnesses deny that modern man can receive the apostolic gifts of divine healing and speaking in tongues. Their rivals in the mission fields often claim possession of such gifts: the Pentecostalists, Assemblies of God, Foursquare Gospelers.

In the familiar sectarian spirit the Witnesses object to any religious titles such as Father, Reverend, or Bishop. They condemn the use of creeds such as the Apostles', Nicene and Athanasian. They find abhorrent the use of images, crucifixes, and relics of saints.

The only day in the year which holds any special significance for them is the 14th of Nisan when they gather to observe the Lord's Evening Meal. They will have nothing to do with Lent or Easter.

Witness authors—now all anonymous—sprinkle their books and tracts with hundreds of proof texts. Unless the writings are addressed to nonbelievers the authors quote their own productions of the Christian Greek Scriptures and Hebrew Scriptures. The individual Witness gets no encouragement to take up his Bible and interpret it for himself. The Watchtower Society, Jehovah's own, does this for him and keeps him from falling into the errors of false religion. The Society explains the many differences between its current theology and that of Russell and Rutherford as the result of progressively greater mastery of the Scriptures. The impression held by the Witness-in-the-pew probably differs little from that of his Roman Catholic adversary. Both believe that God preserves the church authorities from error in interpreting the Gospel.

Witnesses base their apologetics on a belief in God and in the authority and infallibility of the Bible. The agnostic who rejects belief in both will find few attempts at proof in Watchtower publications. Nowhere does the Society try to "prove" the existence of Jehovah God as does St. Thomas Aquinas in his five proofs. As for the authority of the Bible, the Witness says only that its inner harmony and the loftiness of its message guarantee its inspiration.

At one time the aggressive Arian heresy nearly succeeded in capturing the young Christian Church. Its chief doctrinal innovation was the denial of the divinity of Christ. Later Islam wiped out the Christian Church in North Africa and one of its potent weapons was the utter simplicity of its formula: "There is no God but Allah and Mohammed is His prophet." The difficult and subtle doctrine of the Trinity of Father, Son and Holy Ghost confuses many prospective converts to Christianity. Its accurate definition by a Christian believer is rare.

On a theological level the New World Society presents a system that has much the same appeal as Arianism and Islam. It rejects whatever cannot be rationally explained, starting with the Trinity which Christians call a mystery of faith. It dispenses with the doctrine of an eternal hell, which was a novel position in American Christianity when Pastor Russell began his preaching mission in the 1870's though many moderns have implicity rejected the doctrine. It offers a purely natural happiness right here in a paradisical earth to the great majority of mankind, which it contrasts with the popular vision of a heaven of harps and pearly gates. Islam still holds a few trump cards in the battle for black Africa: it condones polygamy and promises a bevy of houris in the afterlife which the Watchtower cannot match.

6. *Inside Kingdom Hall*

FOR THE DEDICATED WITNESS OF JEHOVAH, life revolves around his door-to-door preaching and the four weekly meetings in his Kingdom Hall. Local meeting places which other denominations call churches, synagogues or temples have been known as Kingdom Halls since the first Honolulu hall by that name was dedicated in 1935.

Some of the more than 4,330 Kingdom Halls in the United States are still no more than store fronts or tiny rented halls at the other end of Main Street. But more and more congregations are erecting modest but comfortable and sometimes contemporary-styled halls.

For years the congregation of Jehovah's Witnesses in Lafayette, Indiana (population 35,000), had met in a converted store between a sheet metal shop and a fundamentalist gospel mission. Last year they built a handsome Kingdom Hall in an outlying residential area. The brothers of the congregation pitched in to dig the foundation, finish the electrical work, install the plumbing, paint the walls. They worked two or three hours a night, four or five on Saturdays, and still kept up their doorstep preaching and Bible meetings. The only labor which was not donated was that needed for laying the concrete blocks. Cost of land, labor and materials: $12,000.

One of the brothers, an architect, drew up the functional design which includes on one floor a 120-seat auditorium, literature counter, library, office, rest rooms and furnace room. The Lafayette congregation now meets in quarters which are the envy of the other 19 congregations in their circuit.

Kingdom Hall is the scene of at least four one-hour meetings every week of the year, but for Jehovah's Witnesses the annual Lord's Evening Meal on Nisan 14 is the high point of the calendar. It holds the same sort of meaning as Christmas and Easter hold for orthodox Christians. Even backsliders and fellow travelers who never show up at the weekly meeting make a special effort to attend this service. Worldwide, as many as 1,500,000 people may attend this communion service although fewer than 13,000—the remnant—would actually receive communion.

By 7 P.M. some of the early arrivals at the Lafayette Kingdom Hall had started to take their seats in the auditorium. The service was scheduled to begin at 8 P.M. Instructions from Brooklyn specify that all congregations hold this service sometime after 6 P.M. A number of women wore Easter-type bonnets and a few displayed orchids and corsages.

Across the stage in cut-out letters was the text for the year assigned by the Watchtower Society: IN UNITY I SHALL SET THEM, LIKE A FLOCK IN THE PEN—Mic. 2:12. Drapes on traverse rods conceal not the Holy of Holies but a chart and blackboard, as befits a basically activist religion. This "Service Chart" is standard equipment in all Kingdom Halls; it shows the number of active publishers (doorstep preachers), magazines sold, average number of home Bible studies in progress, etc. The congregational servant will draw the drapes and refer to the chart during the weekly service meetings. Two potted ferns, two chairs, and a piano complete the stage furniture. Of course, the Witnesses do not allow an American flag in their hall.

Tonight, however, something had been added. On a small table in the middle of the platform was a bottle of red burgundy wine and a plate of unleavened bread slices.* There were also four goblets.

The hall began to fill. Regular members gently chided some of the rarely-seens while the latter tried to explain that their absences were due to sickness, business, travel, and so forth. Well-scrubbed boys and girls sat quietly while their parents visited fellow Witnesses. The Witnesses sponsor no Sunday schools for the children; young and old attend the same weekly meetings. The Lafayette congregation reports a total of 104 members; by the time the service started we counted more than 150 people, some standing in the rear.

The personable congregational servant or overseer, W. A. Miner, introduced me to a number of the brothers: the architect, an IBM supervisor at a state university, an X-ray technician, two carpenters, a welder, a farmer, several factory workers. Bill Miner himself grew up in a Witness family and remembers when the local congregation was counted on the fingers of his hands.

The service began on the dot of eight and consisted of a hymn, prayer, 40-minute lecture by Miner explaining the

* The April 1, 1960, issue of *Watchtower* gives the recipe for making unleavened bread. Use one cup of whole wheat flour, mix with 2¼ cups of water. Beat thoroughly and pour batter on frying pan. After slices become firm put them in a baking pan and bake in even oven at 325 degrees until crisp (p. 223).

sect's views on communion, the blessing of the emblems, the distribution, closing prayer and a final hymn. Eight brothers helped to pass the emblems to the congregation. The wine was poured into goblets and a slice of bread was put on a glass dish. Each person silently passed the emblems to the next person.

No one received communion. Only the members of the remnant would dare to eat of the bread or sip the wine. No one in the Lafayette congregation considered himself a member of the remnant, the heaven-destined class of 144,000. They were content to belong to the "other sheep" whose eternal destiny lay in surviving Armageddon and living in peace and happiness on this renewed earth.

Miner had predicted that no one would receive communion. The only possible exception might be a visiting member of the remnant from some other city, or an ignorant guest. He went to some length in his lecture to point out that only the remnant had the right to partake.

No collection plate was passed at this or any other Witness meeting. Contributors put their donations in a box at the back of the auditorium. The brothers took the bread and wine home and consumed it as regular food. As the *Watchtower* explained: "There is nothing particularly sacred about it after the event."[1]

Through the year Kingdom Hall is more of an educational center than a place of worship in the commonly accepted meaning of the term. Jehovah's Witnesses pay no attention to youth programs, Sunday schools, Boy and Girl Scouts, church suppers, dances, men's breakfasts, ladies aid societies. Each Witness is expected to attend four or five congregational meetings each week, study the Bible and Watchtower literature at home, devote as much time as he can to the door-to-door work. "The average minister in a congregation spends some ten hours monthly in such evangelizing." [2] In this way the Society attempts to train and mold articulate, committed, zealous Witnesses of Jehovah.

Although the Witnesses themselves are embarking on more extensive formal training programs at Brooklyn and Gilead, they look with undisguised disdain on theological seminaries. They point out that Jesus and his apostles never set foot in a seminary but spent their lives defending themselves from the attacks of seminary-trained scribes, Pharisees and Sadducees. (The orthodox Christian might add that the physicians of Jesus' day did not attend accredited medical schools but that most Witnesses would rather have their appendix removed by an M.D. than a correspondence-school doctor.)

The Witnesses believe that their systematic after-hours training in their own Kingdom Halls far surpasses that of accredited seminaries and Bible colleges. "Paul did not point to some diploma from one of the theological schools of his time or to any other human authorization when his status as a minister was challenged," states the Jehovah's Witnesses minister's manual.[3]

One of the four weekly meetings in Kingdom Halls is the Sunday afternoon public lecture. This is often advertized by handbills passed out on street corners, especially if the speaker comes from Brooklyn or some other congregation. Sometimes the talk is given by the overseer himself or a fluent Witness. The Witness sponsors naturally hope that some of those who attend out of curiosity will be attracted to enroll in a Bible study class.

Speakers are instructed to follow as closely as possible the outline furnished by Brooklyn. "This [public meeting] talk is primarily for persons of the general public and those of good will, and they need the simple milk of God's Word, not being able yet to stand the strong meat of the deeper things of God."[4] The minister's guide also warns: "[The speaker] will avoid use of slang, vulgarity or lower forms of expression. One can overbalance a speech by being too humorous or by using too much nontheocratic material."[5]

Speaker at the June 11, 1961, public meeting at the Lafayette Kingdom Hall was Robert Walders, congregational servant of the Attica, Indiana, group. He had once been a pioneer in the Lafayette area and knew most of the Lafayette brothers and sisters. His talk was called "The March of World Powers in Prophecy." Miner welcomed the visitors and Witnesses and introduced the speaker.

Walders launched into an involved discussion of the identities of the beasts and demons in the Book of Daniel, culminating in a denunciation of the United Nations as the "wild beast" of prophecy and child of the seventh world power, the Anglo-American empire.

The mercury had reached 91 that Sunday and by 6 P.M. the Hall was still stuffy and humid. Children squirmed on the theatre-type seats. One mother twice hauled her three-year-old boy into the ladies' room at the side of the auditorium and administered a rousing spanking to quiet his whining. Several older Witnesses clucked in disapproval. The lecture lasted a full 60 minutes. There was no question period but Miner invited inquirers to discuss their problems with any Witness.

Miner declared an intermission before proceeding with the second meeting of the evening, the *Watchtower* study. Witnesses gathered around the literature counter at the rear of the hall to pick up new books and magazines, fill out service reports, exchange gossip.

This meeting began at 7:30 P.M. with a hymn and prayer. About two thirds of those at the public lecture stayed for the second half of the evening's program. Each issue of the *Watchtower* carries two articles which include a number of questions on content. These four articles a month serve as pegs for discussion in the study meeting. Participants are expected to have read the articles beforehand. The manual states: "It is assumed that all have studied the lesson in advance and know the answers as contained in the paragraphs." [6] The *Watchtower* study servant read the question for the first paragraph of the article and asked for answers. A dozen hands shot into the air and he called on several members for comments. The Witnesses invariably refer to each other as "Brother" and "Sister." The children got their opportunity to respond and some as young as seven and eight offered concise answers. Some of the paragraphs referred to scriptural passages and the servant called on various members to read these passages. Most Witnesses thumbed Bibles as well as the magazine. Finally the servant asked his assistant on the platform to read the paragraph from the magazine.

Like the other Kingdom Hall sessions, this one lasted just one hour and closed with prayer. The method was mechanical but no more so than the traditional catechetical system of traditional churches. Most members simply gave back what they had read in the magazine but a few introduced a touch of humor, an illustrative example from their doorstep preaching, a homely example.

On Thursdays the Lafayette congregation holds its other two general meetings: the theocratic ministry school and the service meeting. The theocratic ministry school was inaugurated in 1943 by President Knorr. The aim of the program is not so much theological as forensic. It seeks to turn out polished platform speakers. The doctrine they get from the other Kingdom Hall meetings.

The school consists of six parts. First the instructor reviews the work of the previous week. Then he gives a short instruction talk. Three student presentations of about eight minutes each are then delivered and criticized. Finally the audience is invited to participate with comments and questions. This program of bootstrap education has succeeded in turning a tiny band of robots who toted phonographs and printed testimonial cards into an army of confident, persuasive, well-informed Witnesses.

The theocratic ministry school uses only volunteer teachers, charges no tuition, holds no graduations. All Witnesses may enroll although at one time women were excluded. The school servant keeps enrollment charts and drops those who miss too many classes.

Members get their assignments several weeks in advance to prepare the model talks. They may use source material from Watchtower publications, the Bible and personal experiences. The instructor takes about two minutes to comment on delivery, gestures, use of illustrations. Women may ask questions but may not offer criticism of a male speaker. This training goes on week after week, year after year. As one result, many Witnesses who may never have received a high school diploma put most college graduates in the shade on the rostrum.

To schedule more model speeches the Lafayette group splits this part of the program into two sections. One meets in the auditorium and the other in the library. One of the speakers was a lad of about thirteen. His topic: "Satan's Comeuppance." In order to abide by St. Paul's advice that women remain silent in the churches, the Witnesses allow women to speak only in demonstrations of doorstep techniques. One sister takes the part of the householder while the other is a Witness. Two other sisters enact a back call demonstration.

The overseer bears most of the responsibility for the successful service meeting, the fourth type of Kingdom Hall meeting. At this meeting the congregation takes up the mechanics of preaching, magazine quotas, assignment of territories, organization of home Bible classes, handling of back calls. The overseer receives a monthly guide, the *Informant.* He assigns other roles to fellow Witnesses as discussion leaders, panelists, speakers.

The Lafayette service meeting follows the theocratic ministry school after a brief intermission. Members use as their text *Preaching and Teaching in Peace and Unity,* an intramural publication whose circulation is limited to baptized Witnesses. The topic for the evening happened to be disfellowshiping. Like all sects the Watchtower tries to weed out the sinners from the saints. Members observing other Witnesses carrying on with women in an unseemly manner, frequenting taverns, shirking home responsibilities and such are asked to report such misconduct to the congregational service committee. The committee may counsel with the erring one and put him or her on probation or even exclude him from the fellowship.

Another Witness meeting, the congregation book study, may be held in either Kingdom Hall or in the homes of members. This meeting is usually scheduled for Sunday morning. It is designed to entice nonbelievers who might hesitate to visit the hall or who may live at some distance from the hall. As the Watchtower study group uses the semimonthly magazine as its text, so the book study group relies on the various bound books issued by the Society.

Fundamentally all these meetings aim at preparing effective home missionaries who can bring in the "other sheep" who will in turn enter the same training program. Stress is laid on persuasive speaking, memorization of Bible proof texts, tie-ins with current events, answers to stock objections. Motivation and involvement are high; tomorrow the Witness may be able to use what he learned at Kingdom Hall tonight to answer an inquirer.

Witnesses do not stalk converts in any haphazard or hit-and-miss fashion. They follow a systematic program of involvement to bring others into the New World Society. Perhaps this seven-step program has best been outlined by an ex-Witness of 30 years' standing in Germany and the United States. He is William J. Schnell, author of *Thirty Years a Watch Tower Slave* and *Into the Light of Christianity*.

Step No. 1 is to get a Watchtower book or magazine into the hands of the householder. Each doorstep sermon concludes with an offer of a Watchtower book. The price is small; many people will pay 50 cents for a 300-page bound book with illustrations, possibly in color. Others consider their contribution as simply a gift to a religious organization. Some may toss some coins to the persistent Witness in order to get back to their TV show or afternoon nap. If the householder balks at buying the book the Witness will usually produce a copy of the magazine which sells for only a nickel.

The second step is the "back call" designed to encourage the purchaser to read and study the book he has bought. Once upon a time the Watchtower publisher thought he had done his duty in selling the book itself but by the end of the 1920's the organization was urging all publishers to follow up these sales. All back calls are carefully tabulated in the Service Chart and the Publisher's Weekly Field Service Report.

Thirdly, the publisher tries to get the purchaser to agree to attend a weekly home study session on the book he has bought. He also urges the prospect to subscribe to the *Watchtower* and *Awake!* (each sells for only $1 a year for 26 issues) and to order other books which would further explain the New World Society.

Gradually the outsider is being drawn into the organization. The fourth step is to invite him to join one of the congregation or area book studies. Here he meets other active Witnesses and engages in the carefully controlled dialogue by which Witnesses assimilate Watchtower material. The prospective convert by this time should begin to think like a Witness of Jehovah and to view the old world and its problems with some disgust.

As the fifth step the prospect is asked to attend the *Watchtower* study in Kingdom Hall. Potential converts are warmly welcomed by the brethren and shown how they can soon go out themselves to preach to others what they have learned. By this time they may now regard their former church homes, if any, as simply part of Satan's empire. They are told they are highly privileged to enter the ark of the New World Society in which they will be able to ride out the imminent battle of Armageddon.

Next they are asked to help bring in other people of good will by calling on their neighbors even as someone called on them, perhaps many months ago. But to prepare themselves for this they would have to attend the regular service meetings. Here they would learn all they need to know to carry on this work.

The neophyte publisher must learn how to fill out the detailed reports demanded by Brooklyn. For example, the house-to-house record uses various symbols to indicate the warmth of the responses: *I* (interested), *CA* (call again), *B* (busy), *NH* (not home), *NI* (not interested), *OP* (opposed). Each week the publisher must submit his field service report listing total number of books and magazines sold, hours of doorstep preaching, subscriptions obtained, back calls made.

Not every convert is an extrovert. Many are terrified at the thought of calling at some stranger's door and delivering a sermonette. They need a pat on the back from an older Witness. They probably begin this work by accompanying an experienced publisher as a silent partner. Eventually they will gain enough confidence to add a few words. By repeating a simple message often enough they are also making Watchtower dogmas a part of their own personality.

They will discover that their home town is divided into territories and that each publisher is assigned a specific area. The diligent Witness tries to call on each household in his territory at least three times a year. Obviously this is sometimes impossible in a large city with a small congregation of Jehovah's Witnesses.

Finally, the convert is ready for the seventh and last step: baptism. After a period as a publisher including "solo flights," the convert is gently reminded that he must now symbolize his dedication to Jehovah by undergoing baptism by immersion. The Witnesses see no sacramental meaning in the rite of baptism; it is a symbol that the convert is now fully committed to the service of Jehovah God and the building of the New World Society.

These baptisms are usually held during circuit assemblies or international assemblies. They may use an indoor or outdoor swimming pool or beach. The baptized Witness now qualifies in the eyes of the Brooklyn Vatican as a full-fledged Kingdom publisher. He has thrown in his lot with Jehovah's

Witnesses and one by one has snipped the ties which once bound him to the secular community.

No wonder that the Watchtower usually commands the lifelong loyalty of its converts. This patient, individualistic indoctrination is a far cry from the spur-of-the-moment decision for Christ at a Billy Graham revival or the socially oriented membership in a suburban church. During 1961 the Society reported an average of 1,900 hours were spent in preaching and 400 back calls were recorded for each convert. This indoctrination may continue for many months before the convert comes to stand in his bathing suit waiting for immersion.

The fact that this program of gradual involvement extends for so many months also leads us to believe that, though the Watchtower membership is listed as 900,000, the total number of Witnesses and "fellow travelers" or catechumens may already have reached 1,500,000. The attendance of 1,500,000 at the annual communion service indicates to some degree the number of those who consider Kingdom Hall to be their spiritual home. The huge magazine circulations (approaching 4,000,000 for the *Watchtower*) may also mean that three or four people get a regular dose of Watchtower doctrine for each Witness subscriber.

Dedicated publishers get eminently practical tips on how to carry on their ministry. The minister's manual, *Qualified to Be Ministers,* gives suggestions on speech preparation, use of proof texts, different approaches to men and women householders, angles to take with Catholics, Protestants and Jews. The book explains that the publisher may introduce himself at the door as a minister, a representative of the Watchtower Society (not many people recognize the corporate name), or an educator affiliated with "an international Bible research group." If he is trying to sell the New World Translation of the Bible he can say he "represents a Bible translation committee." No veteran Witness would greet the lady of the house with "I'm a Jehovah's Witness."

One of his first objectives, he is told, is to get inside the house. To do this he can sometimes use the discomfort of the householder as a lever. If it is snowing or raining he can suggest that it would be better if he stepped inside to explain his purpose, allowing his host to close the door against the elements.

If a man answers the door the discussion might begin with remarks about the world situation: gloomy and getting worse. The alert Witness can usually quote some current headlines to verify the estimate. The conversation is gradually guided toward Armageddon. If a woman answers, the publisher might launch into a more directly religious message. He might get agreement that it is a shame that people do not read and study the Bible as much as they should. Like all good salesmen, he tries to get several affirmative answers to maneuver the propect into a mood of agreement.

After five or six minutes the Witness will bring up the nature of the literature he is selling. The manual states: "Convince the people that the literature is a product of research, not the interpreation of some individuals." [7] The publishers are instructed to mention the expected contribution and to try to get the householder to take the book in his hands. This is half the battle.

If the publisher makes a sale he is instructed to tell the buyer that he is now entitled to a free private lesson on the contents of the book. The ideal is to nail down a specific date and time for the back call at the time of the sale.

Of course, the door-to-door witnessing is not the only form

of proselytizing activity. Some Witnesses prefer to stand on a street corner to sell the magazines. Each Witness receives a 12-copy-per-month quota of each magazine. Some Witnesses call numbers selected at random from a telephone book and try to interest whoever answers. Some Witness shut-ins watch the local obituary notices and write sympathy letters to the bereaved. Naturally these letters express the Watchtower attitudes toward the dead and the last things.

In the inevitable arguments on religion the Witness gets some sound advice. "Get as many agreements as possible from your opponent. Ask questions, get your opponent to commit himself." [8] As the inquirer begins to show some interest he must not be scared off. "Do not tell the good-will person that he will be required by us to quit his religion." [9] Of course, he will; but at the outset many souls receive the impression that all this attention is simply the extension work of a Christian Bible society rather than the initial steps of involvement in one of the world's best-organized cults.

Once baptized, the new publisher may aspire to any one of a number of posts of responsibility in Kingdom Hall. The top job is that of congregational overseer or servant. He is ordinarily a mature, well-grounded brother. He gets his instructions from Brooklyn and from the circuit servant and passes them on to those in his charge.

Helping the overseer are eight assistants. They are the assistant congregational servant, the Bible study servant, the magazine territory servant, the literature servant, the accounts servant, the Watchtower study servant, the theocratic ministry servant, and the book study servant. These added duties do not relieve them of meeting the same quota of preaching hours and sales as other members. No one receives any salary for these jobs although all publishers get a small discount on publications. Almost all these congregational officials also hold down 40-hour-a-week secular jobs.

In any congregation there may also be full-time personnel known as pioneers. These may be retired people, housewives, or "career" Witnesses who spend practically all their time preaching. Pioneers get a small allowance from headquarters and should log at least 100 hours a month, while special pioneers must put in 150 hours. Their hours do not appear on the local service chart; they report directly to Brooklyn.

Each congregation belongs to a circuit of 18 to 20 congregations under the supervision of a circuit servant. He tries to visit each congregation three times a year. Most of the 257 circuit servants are married and either live in trailers or with families in the congregation who also supply food and other necessities. Bethel picks up the transportation tab. A number of circuits make up a district; districts combine to form a branch (usually an entire nation); and branches make up ten global zones.

Witness policy is to keep congregations small. Before a congregation reaches 200 members, the circuit servant will suggest it be split into two. Around the world the Society adds about a dozen new congregations each week.

All Witnesses are asked to make a monetary pledge for the coming year to the Watchtower Society to enable the central office to prepare its budget. This is called the Contribution Prospects. The Witnesses never pass a collection plate, sponsor a bingo party or church supper. Nor do they believe in tithing, weekly envelopes or fund-raising devices. (The last experience with Pastor Russell's Miracle Wheat turned into a disaster.) Of course, the Kingdom Hall has no great expenses outside of utilities and heat. No one draws a salary. The Hall does not attempt to operate a school system as do

Catholic and Lutheran parishes. Witnesses need not worry about supporting related church institutions such as colleges, hospitals, homes for the aged, orphanages, clinics and the like. "We do not operate hospitals or clinics any more than we run fire departments or police forces, which also preserve life and limb," explains President Knorr.[10]

Ideally each publisher will put in 60 hours a month in doorstep or street-corner preaching. Actually the average in most congregations comes closer to 11 or 12 hours. Some naturally lose their zeal, some are ill, some hold jobs which rule out normal preaching. The Society does claim, however, that two thirds of the members attend at least four classes a week in Kingdom Hall.

Women may serve as ministers in the New World Society but the Society also draws on St. Paul and tradition to maintain male supremacy in the congregations. No women may hold a teaching post, deliver public lectures, or direct the activities of the brothers. "Sisters should not try to give counsel to the dedicated brothers. On this matter they are 'to be in silence.' They must not argue with or contradict them or give instructions." [11] The sisters are especially warned against gossiping and backbiting in the congregation.

The Society believes that even children may qualify as ministers of the gospel. Some sell magazines on the streets. Some accompany their parents or older Witnesses in the door-to-door calls. They participate in all the meetings in Kingdom Hall. They are told to "avoid worldly associations, ties and obligations." [12] If they should wonder about the propriety of getting involved in any particular school activity they should consult their parents if they are "in the truth" or some mature member of the congregation. Above all they must keep themselves free from contamination with the children of the world. A recent *Watchtower* counsels: "Some of you have the bad habit of repeatedly running out to the rest rooms during meetings. You, no doubt, acquired this habit from the juvenile delinquents with whom you are obliged to rub elbows in the public schools and who use it as a means to give expression to their frustration and rebellion. Beware of imitating them!" [13] The dedicated Witness couple will pray that their children may follow the vocation of pioneer or foreign missionary for the Society.

Each Witness calls on an average of ten homes a week. He has learned to expect rebuffs, slammed doors, insults, apathy. But he knows that despite the opposition, his New World Society is growing at an amazing rate. He can share his preaching experiences with his brothers and sisters in Kingdom Hall. He enjoys a warm fellowship with anywhere from a dozen to 200 fellow Witnesses of Jehovah. He feels secure within the walls of the Kingdom Hall he may have helped to build with his own hands.

With the patience of Job and the persistence of a life insurance agent, the Witness publisher is making modern religious history. No contemporary religious movement begins to match the degree of lay participation (except perhaps Mormonism), thoroughness of converts' indoctrination, or rate of growth of Jehovah's Witnesses.

So the faithful Witness of Jehovah serves Jehovah. He probably holds down a full-time secular job, attends four or five classes a week in Kingdom Hall, participates in a Bible study group, and tries to devote his spare hours to doorstep preaching. No wonder he encounters few temptations to reevaluate the New World Society and even fewer to pursue vain and worldly ambitions.

7. *The Vatican in Brooklyn*

POWERHOUSE for the burgeoning New World movement is a complex of buildings in the fashionable Columbia Heights section of Brooklyn, New York. Here more than 700 men and women, including all the officers of the Watchtower Bible and Tract Society, live and work. From here orders are sent to the 85 branch offices around the globe.

The original Bethel (a Hebrew word meaning House of God) was built on the site of the Beecher parsonage at 124 Columbia Heights. The second and larger Bethel Home addition, also overlooking the East River and the lower Manhattan skyline, was dedicated in 1960.

This new building, part of a $4,000,000 expansion program, was begun in 1958 after President Knorr announced at the international assembly that the growth of the Society demanded more living room at headquarters.

To finance the project the Society turned to its traditional method. In a letter dated April 1, 1959, to Jehovah's Witnesses the Society offered promissory notes in return for loans in units of $100 at 3 per cent interest. Similar notes financed building in 1926, 1946 and 1955 and all these prior notes had been paid off. The brethren also made outright gifts for the new Bethel addition.

Visitors to the new building enter through a wrought-iron gate into a courtyard featuring a pool of blue ceramic tile from Italy. The area is landscaped with a variety of trees and formal gardens. Inside Bethel, visitors are treated to a breathtaking view of Manhattan's skyscrapers.

The Watchtower Bible School of Gilead was moved from South Lansing in upstate New York to Brooklyn. The first two floors of the new 11-story Bethel are encased in marble and glass and house the offices of the School, four classrooms, and a large lecture hall. The School's library of 10,000 volumes on the third floor adjoins an outdoor terrace and lounge. Floors three, four and five accommodate the 100 Gilead students from many nations enrolled for the ten-month course. Counting practical work experience in the Watchtower factory and offices, the students spend a full year in Brooklyn.

The remaining floors house the regular Bethel residents, including Mr. and Mrs. Knorr. Others continue to live in the older Bethel across the street. When filled to capacity with two Witnesses to a room the buildings can shelter 1,100 men and women. In 1950 there were only 355 living at Bethel. The ratio of men to women is now about seven to one; no racial distinctions are made in living quarters.

The Kingdom Hall at Bethel seats 750 people and is paneled in walnut. One complete wall along Willow Street is glass. The platform is flanked by planter boxes. Chairs and other furniture in the hall and living quarters were made in Bethel's own basement furniture shop.

The building was built by a construction firm but Witnesses pitched in to help and trim costs. The structural engineer for concrete-and-steel reinforced framework was a Jehovah's Witness. Witnesses handled much of the plumbing and steamfitting. Others worked as line and grade men, timekeepers, watchmen, painters, tile and carpet layers. Eighty brothers in the New York area responded to a call for cleanup volunteers. By means of such contributed labor the Society cut thousands of dollars off the estimated cost.

Bethel is a small city with its own barber and beauty shops, laundry, dry cleaning plant, kitchens, shoe repair shop, furniture factory, library, infirmary, Kingdom Hall. A registered nurse and a chiropractor care for the health of the residents.

Much of its food including all dairy products comes from the Society's farms in South Lansing, New York, and Port Murray, New Jersey. The 800-acre South Lansing farm is worked by 46 people. Counting the farm workers, Bethel residents and approximately 200 students, the Society feeds 900 people a day. By raising much of its own food and employing various economies it can feed each person on an average of 54 cents a day, 18 cents a meal.

A monastic spirit pervades the house. A bell rouses residents at 6:30 A.M. They bathe, dress and assemble for morning devotions. Tables for ten are set up in the common refectory and the meals are presided over by Knorr if he is in town. Morning devotions consist of a hymn, prayer and grace before meals. The day's Bible text from the *Yearbook* is read and discussed at breakfast. Knorr or a stand-in may decide to quiz some of the residents and ask them by name to explain parts of the text. The meal itself is finished in ten minutes.

By eight o'clock the Witnesses are ready to start their day's work as linotypists, pressmen, bindery workers, supervisors, writers, translators, typists, artists, secretaries, mail clerks, etc. They put in eight hours and 40 minutes a day, five and a half days a week. Most of the residents walk to the factory buildings about six blocks away.

The Witnesses often take a farm boy from Kansas or North Dakota, give him two or three months' training as a pressman, and let him take charge of a $250,000 rotary press. As a union apprentice and journeyman it might take him 10 years to reach this responsibility.

I have never seen young men work harder or more cheerfully at their jobs than the compositors, linotypists, pressmen, bindery, shipping and mailing workers at the Watchtower factory. You find no malingering, no pin-up pictures on the walls, no scraps of paper on the floor. Every scrap of wastepaper is collected and baled and the factory realizes more than $1,000 a week from its sale.

Many of the machines used in the binding and mailing operations were designed and manufactured by Witnesses themselves. Witness mechanics, electricians, carpenters, keep the plant in running order. No non-Witnesses are employed. Besides being a huge factory the Watchtower plant is also a school of the graphic arts. Not a few of the young men who learn the printing trade here finish their three- or four-year hitches and return home to take well-paying jobs in secular printing plants.

At noon and evening meals the dinner-table conversation is directed toward scriptural topics. The five regular congregational meetings are held in Bethel's Kingdom Hall although residents also belong to congregations scattered throughout the New York area. They try to put in their expected quota of door-to-door calls on Saturday afternoons and Sunday. By 10:30 P.M. another bell signals lights out.

Once every two or three weeks a Bethel resident will take a night off to attend a lecture or concert.

Most but not all of the residents are unmarried. The use of alcohol, tobacco and profanity is discouraged. All residents of Bethel from President Knorr down to the greenest secretarial recruit from Kansas get the same recompense: room, board and $14 a month allowance for clothing and incidental expenses. An annual bonus averaging $5 a month is distributed according to years of seniority as Bethel residents. It can be spent for clothing and dry cleaning. Once asked by a newspaper reporter how he managed on such a budget, Knorr replied, "I have been told it's impossible to get along on $14 a month. It's not. It's easy when the necessities like food and lodging are provided. When I travel my expenses are paid by the office."

Applicants for Bethel must be between seventeen and thirty-five and agree to sign up for a minimum of three years. Most of the workers appear to be in their twenties and thirties. There is a waiting list of Witnesses who want to devote their full time to the work.

At the factory at 117 Adam Street the Society operates one of the most modern and efficient printing plants in the United States. Here 11 huge rotary and two flatbed presses turn out the tens of millions of books, magazines and tracts which the Witnesses use to spread their message of Armageddon and the New World. The 30,000 bound books turned out every working day of the year at the Brooklyn factory would make a stack almost twice as tall as the Empire State Building.

Before 1919 the Society bought its printing from various commercial printers. After this date they entered the printing business themselves and occupied a succession of small buildings until they built the original 8-story factory on Adams Street. They later added a 4-story and a 9-story addition and thought these would take care of their publishing needs for many years. But they soon outgrew these facilities. The Society completed the 13-story factory in 1956. It was built across the street from the original plant but is connected by an overhead bridge.

Skilled Witnesses not only set the type and run the presses but manufacture the engravings, electrotypes, and inks. They buy their paper from secular paper mills but can realize substantial savings because of the huge quantities they order.

Some idea of the expansion of the Brooklyn printing operation can be seen by consulting the 1956 and the 1962 *Yearbooks*. In 1956 the plants printed 36,500,383 copies of *Watchtower* and *Awake!* Five years later the plant turned out 61,071,030 copies of the *Watchtower* and another 54,040,200 copies of *Awake!*

Each magazine makes its special appeal. The *Watchtower* is written for the dedicated Witness and assumes a knowledge of the doctrines and vocabulary of the New World Society. Its articles are generously larded with Scripture references and include questions for use in the weekly Watchtower study session in Kingdom Halls. *Awake!* tries to appeal to the casually interested who may have contributed a nickel only to get rid of the Witness at the door. Typical articles in recent months have been "Snoring: Plight of the Night," "Fill the Room with Music [stereo]," "The Sensitive Sense of Smell," and "Are You Troubled with Constipation?" It seeks only to whet the reader's appetite for more information about Jehovah's Witnesses.

Similar but smaller Bethels have been built in dozens of branch centers. More than 1,300 Bethel residents around the world live in these semimonastic communities. Some Bethels are substantial buildings, such as those serving England, Germany and Canada. Many homes are run in conjunction with a printing plant. This contributed labor and the tremendous quantities of the press runs explain how the Society is able to sell its books for only 75 cents and its magazines for a nickel a copy.

Bethel Home may be a far cry from a Trappist or Benedictine monastery but provides some parallels. It furnishes a core of skilled, dedicated workers for the expansion of the New World Society. If it makes no demands of celibacy it expects obedience and practically guarantees poverty.

8. *When Good Witnesses Get Together*

JEHOVAH'S WITNESSES love to go to conventions. These meetings of the New World Society serve more than strictly religious purposes. They serve psychological and public relations purposes as well.

Only one American out of 702 is a Witness of Jehovah. Many congregations are tiny assemblies and even in a medium-sized city Witnesses may find only a few score fellow believers. But they cannot keep their religion to themselves. Week after week they tramp from door to door. Relatively few of their neighbors show any interest in their life-or-death message and veteran Witnesses have lost count of the insults and doors slammed shut in their faces.

Circuit, district and international assemblies periodically show the isolated Witness that he does not stand alone. Hundreds and thousands and even hundreds of thousands of others share his faith. He meets fellow Witnesses who are friendly, dedicated, enthusiastic. They share preaching experiences. The fellowship of the assembly renews morale and builds pride in the accomplishments and growth of the Society.

For example, almost 1,000 Witnesses attended a typical circuit assembly in a small Indiana farming community recently. They came from 20 congregations in Indiana and Illinois for the three-day semiannual convention. Most delegates arranged to stay with householders in a nearby city; local Witnesses had canvassed the vicinity for spare rooms weeks before the first session.

Angelo C. Manera, Jr., a former Roman Catholic from Brooklyn who is now a district supervisor for the circuit, delivered the opening address Friday evening in the high school auditorium-gymnasium. Later he conducted a model theocratic ministry school similar to those held weekly in all Kingdom Halls. Manera, handsome and well dressed, knew most of the delegates personally since it is his job to visit the 20 congregations under his direction and serve as the representative of the Society.

Saturday morning the visiting Witnesses reported to assigned neighborhoods to blanket the area with house-to-house calls. They distributed copies of the *Watchtower* and handbills advertising their convention. Later in the day they heard Manera deliver a sermon on "Dedication and Baptism" which preceded the baptism of converts in a YMCA pool. In the evening the public was invited to join the Witnesses to see a film about the 1958 Divine Will International Assembly in New York City.

Climaxing this fall meeting was an open lecture featuring Manera in a talk entitled "When Is God's Will to Be Done on Earth?" Not only did the Witnesses pass out thousands of handbills but they inserted publicity stories in local newspapers, mounted placards on their automobiles, and put posters in downtown store windows.

About 1,200 people jammed the gymnasium, usually

packed with screaming Hoosier basketball fans. The crowd exceeded the total population of the village and would probably be recalled by the natives for years afterward. Most of these people were Witnesses but the audience included curious villagers, high school students, landladies who rented rooms to Witness delegates, people invited Saturday morning. Several of the women were quite attractive and, unlike many fundamentalists, the Witnesses do not scorn fur pieces, cosmetics and stylish frocks and coats. The audience included a sprinkling of Negroes.

A 12-piece band, horribly off beat, entertained the crowd waiting for the 3 P.M. lecture. A gaudily painted backdrop on the stage depicted an earthly paradise at the end of a rainbow where a family group played with tame lions and wolves near a rose-covered cottage.

At precisely three o'clock Manera approached the rostrum. He read his entire speech. His jokes drew hearty laughter and the audience interrupted several times with applause. The spontaneous "Amen" and "Praise Be to Jesus" interjections at the usual revival service were missing.

The speaker painted a frightening portrait of modern society beset by H-bombs, juvenile delinquency, corruption in high places, overpopulation. Manera picked examples from current newspapers—almost any issue would do. Mankind's best efforts to restore order in this old world drew sarcastic comments and predictions of futility. The speaker labeled the United Nations a "tombstone of failure." He ridiculed the orthodox churches which still preach that the wicked will "sizzle and fry, roast and toast" in an eternal hell. The Witnesses chuckled.

How can mankind escape Armageddon, the climax of all these evils? By fleeing to the ark of the New World Society as so many have done. A sociologist would have spotted the speaker's frequent use of the bandwagon technique as he recounted the story of the remarkable growth of the Watchtower Society, the size of its publishing operation, the attendance at the 1958 assembly, etc. He invited non-Witnesses of good will to welcome Witnesses to their homes, begin Bible studies, buy and read Watchtower books.

At the end of the one-hour talk the audience headed for the exits, the Witnesses to attend specialized meetings or get ready for supper. No collection plate was passed but contribution boxes were set up at the entrance to each aisle. By eight o'clock most of the Witnesses would be heading home to secular jobs in the Old World Society.

Witnesses look forward to these circuit assemblies as a combination spiritual experience and vacation. They serve somewhat the same purpose as the camp meeting or Chautauqua of traditional Protestantism. During the week of the assembly all activities at Kingdom Halls in the area are suspended; some congregations regularly send 75 per cent of their members to these meetings. By traveling in car pools, staying in private homes and eating most meals in cafeterias manned by Witness cooks and waiters, they can cut costs to a minimum.

During the summer months the Society schedules assemblies which draw representations from larger geographical territories. For example, during 1961 there were 12 assemblies in the United States, Canada and Europe.

Just before the start of the 1961 district assembly in New York City the Jesuit weekly *America* carried an article warning "unprepared Catholics" against engaging in Bible debates with Jehovah's Witnesses. The author of the article, Albert Muller, wrote:

The Jehovah's Witnesses are specialists in their own peculiar way. In general, they know more about the Bible than most Catholics. Since they insist on carrying on all discussions on the basis of the Bible, a Catholic involved with them will be forced to meet them on their own grounds. While the Witnesses' view of the Bible is a distorted one, the deplorable lack of knowledge that a Catholic is likely to have of the Holy Scriptures puts him at a serious disadvantage.[1]

Writer Muller, a Catholic street preacher and one of the founders of Christ's Witnesses, a group of laymen who try to counter Jehovah's Witnesses proselytizing among Roman Catholics, concluded:

It would be well to advise unprepared Catholics to avoid them [Jehovah's Witnesses], for they will accomplish little and may endanger their own faith. Only well instructed Catholics can cope with them.[2]

To this President Knorr retorted: "If just a visit of Jehovah's Witnesses can change a Catholic's faith, it is proof that the Catholic clergy are not giving to their people proper training in the Bible." Needling the Catholic magazine a bit more, he added: "When we go to them, why don't they train people to convert us to being Catholic? If they had the truth, and went out, and witnessed to it, they would be able to convert the world in two or three years—they have enough people to do it." Finally, he charged that the Catholics "preach a tradition they have made up and carried over from pagan rituals."

About 40,000 Witnesses were on hand for the opening of the six-day district assembly at Yankee Stadium, June 20–25. The committee put 2,400 potted geraniums around the lecture platform on second base. They erected eight huge tents to serve as restaurants which would be able to feed 500 people a minute. Top price for a full-course meal: 65 cents. Full-time pioneers were fed free.

Across the Harlem River in Manhattan, Spanish-speaking Witnesses held their own assembly in the New Rockland Palace, a garish ballroom on West 155th Street. The Los Testigos de Jehovah drew almost 900 Witnesses to their daily sessions.

Although the main district meeting was designed to serve Witnesses on the eastern seaboard it attracted delegates from 44 states and many foreign countries. Branch manager of the Watchtower for the United States, Milton G. Henschel, drew a laugh from the first-day crowd when he observed: "It's coming to be an accepted fact that a caller at the door will be either the milkman, the postman, or one of Jehovah's Witnesses. Well, that's good."

Delegates hoped to blanket the Bronx and upper Manhattan in a door-to-door campaign during free hours in the course of the convention. Henschel instructed Witnesses to be sure to leave Watchtower booklets with the householders with whom they were staying in the New York area and with hotel employees. Another speaker urged them to treat all householders courteously, to tell no lies—"not even white ones"—and to keep all promises about return calls.

At one session Brother Knorr repeated warnings against giving or receiving blood transfusions. He hinted that those who received such transfusions might well contract various diseases and transmit them to unborn children. A shudder ran through the crowd of 44,000 when the Watchtower president revealed: "It will probably shock you to learn that the blood of dead people is being transfused into the bodies of hospital patients. But reports from Russia and Spain show that is exactly what is done there; and even in the United States experiments have been conducted with transfusion of cadaver blood."

Knorr addressed the final, widely advertised session on Sunday afternoon. Many of the estimated 89,000 people at Yankee Stadium had to sit on the ground during the hour-and-a-half discourse, since the stadium seats only 67,203. He spoke from a revolving platform in center field protected by a blue plastic umbrella.

As usual he singled out the United Nations for special attack. He said that the 99 nations in the world organization "do not appreciate that by being bound together in the U.N. they are united against God and his kingdom."

Speaking of the East-West power struggle, the Watchtower head said:

"There is no need for the democratic-Western bloc of nations to fear that the Communist bloc will take universal control of the earth. There is no need for the Socialist Communist bloc to worry in fear that the democratic Western bloc of nations will take over world domination.

"The universal rule, including domination of the whole earth, has already been conferred, not on the choice of the democrats, nor on the choice of the Communists, nor on the choice of the neutrals, nor on the choice of any man, but on God's choice of ruler, mankind's Savior, Jesus Christ."

While he spoke, a missionary from the Caribbean and Central America area delivered the same lecture to more than 3,000 Spanish-speaking Witnesses in the rented ballroom.

Another feature of the afternoon was the premiere performance of "The Revelation Suite" composed by two Witnesses and played by the 102-piece orchestra. Immediately after the final message hundreds of shirt-sleeved Witnesses started the mammoth cleanup operation to prepare the Stadium for its next baseball game.

Copenhagen was selected as the site of the first European assembly of the 1961 summer. The *Watchtower* explained: "There [in Copenhagen] we should like to see as many as possible so as to make the Danes, who so studiously have been ignoring the Kingdom message for some time now, sit up and take notice." [3] Lectures were translated simultaneously into Norwegian, Swedish, Finnish, Danish and English. The faithful are urged to attend at least one of these assemblies in addition to the circuit assemblies, since any assembly may well be the final opportunity to get together with the brothers and sisters before Armageddon.

Total attendance at the 1961 regional assemblies exceeded 480,000, while the number of baptisms was reported to be 10,974. Largest of the 13 assemblies was that in New York City where 92,901 people heard Knorr's public address. Two new Watchtower books were unveiled: a one-volume New World translation of the Bible and *"Let Your Name Be Sanctified."*

Of the other meetings, the largest was held at Hamburg, Germany, with 88,338 people at the public lecture and the smallest at Turin, Italy, which attracted 6,372. Other attendance figures were Vancouver, B.C. (28,952), Houston, Texas (21,300), Oklahoma City, Oklahoma (12,744), Omaha, Nebraska (11,528), San Francisco, California (50,213), Milwaukee, Wisconsin (40,552), London, England (48,070), Amsterdam, Holland (23,708), Paris, France (23,004), and Copenhagen, Denmark (33,513).

For a spectacular convention the Society issues a call for an international assembly. New York City has been the scene of three such giant meetings since 1950. At the 1953 assembly the energetic Witnesses set up a tent and trailer city in Plainfield, N. J., about 40 miles from New York City. Almost 50,000 men, women and children were housed in these accommodations which had to be provided with water, sanitary facilities, electricity, and public address systems. The main meeting was held in Yankee Stadium but the programs were relayed to Plainfield by radio.

The last international assembly met in New York City, July 27 to August 3, 1958, and made Billy Graham's revival crowds look puny by comparison. In fact more people attended the assembly than comprise the entire population of a state such as Nevada or Alaska.

The 1958 convention brought the New World Society publicity it could never have afforded to buy. The 7,000 native New York Witnesses hardly rated an occasional item on the back page of a metropolitan newspaper. But when 253,000 people pack both Yankee Stadium and the Polo Grounds for a public religious meeting, the newspapers, wire services, radio and TV stations have to take notice. When almost 200,000 people from all over the world descend on a city, even one as huge and sophisticated as New York, and wear identifying badges, distribute millions of handbills, jam public transportation, commandeer entire hotels and motels, the event cannot be ignored. The Watchtower Society received generous coverage in all the daily newspapers, *The New York Times Magazine Section, Time* and *Newsweek,* the *Christian Century,* the AP, UP and INS, and even a number of Roman Catholic magazines.

The *Watchtower* alerted Witnesses 19 months before the opening of the assembly in New York to begin making travel preparations and saving money. The officials of the Society decided against erecting another tent-trailer city but sought to obtain as many private rooms as possible to help visitors cut living costs. During the spring of 1958 some 13,000 Witnesses scoured the cities in a 100-mile radius to sign up available spare rooms. It took three to four hours of canvassing to obtain each room but by the time July 27 dawned not a single Witness lacked shelter.

They came in more than 20,000 automobiles, two chartered ships from Europe, 65 planes, scores of special trains and buses. Witnesses set up information booths at strategic service stations so that motorists could be given the best route to their accommodations.

Another team placed 12,000 posters in New York store windows. All delegates wore large badges which read GOD'S KINGDOM RULES—IS THE WORLD'S END NEAR? During the course of the assembly they passed out 5,000,000 handbills.

A squad of 6,000 cooks and kitchen helpers prepared meals for as many as 68,000 diners an hour; a cleanup crew of 2,500 picked up every scrap of paper, every apple core, and every candy wrapper at the end of each day's session. Park managers accustomed to the litter of Yankee and Giant baseball fans were frankly amazed.

At the ball parks 40 doctors and 125 nurses, mostly Witnesses themselves, took care of upset stomachs, dizzy spells and children who had munched too many hot dogs.

The Society arranged to transport 7,136 converts ranging in age from nine to eighty-four in 58 buses to Orchard Beach in the Bronx for a mass baptism. Men and women changed into bathing suits and joined one of the 30 lines leading candidates about 75 feet into the water. At the end of each line were three immersers who dipped the new Witnesses into the waters. The Society boasted that this mass baptism eclipsed by more than 4,000 the number baptized on the first Pentecost in 33 A.D.

A typical convention day began at 9 A.M. and lasted until 9 at night. During the early morning hours visiting Witnesses tried their hand at making converts among the blasé Manhattanites. (One result of the assembly has been that the lagging Manhattan district now reports one of the largest percentage growths of any district in the United States.)

After lunch the visitors attended sessions at one of the two ball parks while the speakers shuttled back and forth delivering identical addresses to both audiences. Special language sessions for those who did not understand English too well were arranged; the largest of these were conducted in Spanish, German, and French. Two 100-piece orchestras played between sermons; these ensembles were made up of professional musicians, all Witnesses, drawn from 12 symphony orchestras and 21 popular bands.

Many Witnesses accepted an invitation to journey to Brooklyn and visit the printing plant and Bethel Home. At one session the assembly saw 103 graduates receive their diplomas from the Watchtower Bible School of Gilead. Rain poured down on the graduates standing at home plate but the ceremony continued.

At another session President Knorr surprised the audience of 173,000 by announcing that starting in 1959 the women as well as the men could enroll in the weekly theocratic ministry schools. Here they could practice their six-minute doorstep sermons and yet not violate St. Paul's injunction against women speaking in church. They were told not to try to instruct or correct the brothers.

Most of the delegates to the New York assembly came from the United States and Canada but thousands of others registered from 123 other countries, including 4,822 from Europe. Some Witnesses sold their homes and furniture to raise money to attend; they would remember the 1958 assembly as one of the highpoints of their lives.

Among the veterans was Edith Duff of Australia who had been a Watchtower pioneer since 1914. Lucy Shyian of Montreal had been a nun in a convent 18 months before the assembly, according to the Report of the convention. Now she was applying to become a pioneer. D. Griffiths of South Wales set aside one third of his weekly $7 pension for two years to finance the trip. Hisar Sormin of Indonesia had been chess champion of his country. He used to play poker for as long as 48 hours in a stretch, drank heavily, and helped boss an underworld syndicate. Now he was attending the Jehovah's Witnesses assembly as a congregational servant and pioneer from Djakarta and had finally married the woman with whom he lived who had borne his eight children.

In the last days of the 1958 assembly the brothers and sisters heard a Swiss Witness play a tape recording of underground Witnesses behind the Iron Curtain. The hunted Witnesses sang two hymns in four-part harmony and delivered a message of greeting.

More than 194,000 Witnesses roared approval of a resolution which branded "Christendom's clergy as the most reprehensible class on earth today." In booklet form under the title *How Has Christendom Failed All Mankind?* the resolution was reproduced in print 70 million times.

In general the tidy, friendly Witnesses made a good impression on New Yorkers. This was no American Legion or Shriners' orgy. *The New York Times* commented:

Whatever New Yorkers may think of the Witnesses' theology,

they are unanimous in agreeing that the Witnesses' conduct has been exemplary. . . . Their cleanliness is now almost legendary. A week ago a corps of volunteer Witnesses washed down every seat in the Yankee Stadium. When they leave on Sunday the ball park will be spotless. Three years ago Yankee maintenance men testified that when the Witnesses departed the arena had never been cleaner. In the Times Square area where members of the movement have been passing out tracts, handbills and periodicals, courtesy has been their watchword.[4]

Demonstrating a genuine spirit of fraternal cooperation and a command of logistical know-how garnered from dozens of smaller conventions, the Society successfully managed the largest convention the city of New York had ever seen. (No one in the Society's high command seemed to be upset over the fact that Yankee Stadium is now owned by the Knights of Columbus.)

The Society relies on such assemblies to keep morale high, instill pride, win publicity it could never afford to buy, impress townspeople and landladies, announce new doctrines or changes in practice, unveil new books, and maintain discipline in its far-flung religious empire.

INTERNATIONAL CONVENTIONS OF JEHOVAH'S WITNESSES

Year	Place	Attendance	Number Baptized
1893	Chicago, Ill.	360	20
1904	St. Louis, Mo.	2,000	
1908	Put-in-Bay, Ohio	3,500	363
1911	Mountain Lake Park, Md.	5,000	
1919	Cedar Point, Ohio	8,000	
1922	Cedar Point, Ohio	20,000	
1926	London, England	7,000	
1927	Toronto, Canada	15,000	
1928	Detroit, Mich.	12,000	

Year	Place	Attendance	Number Baptized
1931	Columbus, Ohio	15,000	
1935	Washington, D. C.	20,000	
1938	London, England	150,000	
1939	New York City	67,000	
1940	Detroit, Mich.	79,000	
1942	Cleveland, Ohio	129,000	
1944	Buffalo, N. Y.	140,000	3,503
1946	Cleveland, Ohio	80,000	2,602
1950	New York City	123,000	3,381
1953	New York City	165,000	4,640
1958	New York City	253,000	7,136

9. *Missions and Overseas Expansion*

TO MILLIONS OF PEOPLE around the world Brooklyn has become what Vatican City is to Catholics, Boston to Christian Scientists, and Salt Lake City to Mormons.

Two-thirds of the Witnesses of Jehovah live outside the United States. While the percentage increase of Witnesses in this country stood at 7 per cent in 1961 (more than triple the average Protestant growth), the number of Witnesses in such areas as Brazil went up 17 per cent, France 10 per cent, and Mexico 8 per cent. Some of the tiny countries reported much larger but less significant boosts from 20 to 500 per cent.

The largest concentration of Witnesses outside of the United States continues to be in West Germany. The 1962 *Yearbook* reports an average number of publishers to be 67,814 with a peak during the year of 70,712. This means that about one West German out of every 763 is a baptized Witness and many thousands more would be classified as "fellow travelers" who read Watchtower literature, attend Bible classes, rallies and public meetings.

Outside of the historic Roman Catholic and Lutheran communions the West German state recognizes 65 religious sects. The largest of these is the 500,000-member New Apostolic Church, practically unknown in the United States. The second largest sect is Jehovah's Witnesses, followed in order by the Adventists, Pentecostalists, and Mormons.

Pastor Russell set up the first branch office in Germany on his second European tour in 1903. The work progressed inconspicuously until Hitler came to power in 1933. By then the number of German Witnesses or Bible Students almost equaled the U. S. total of about 20,000. As a matter of fact in 1928 the number of Witnesses was 60 per cent larger in Germany than in the United States (9,700 in Germany, 6,000 in United States). Between 1919 and 1933 the energetic German Witnesses had distributed 48,000,000 books and pamphlets printed in their own plants.

As we have seen, Judge Rutherford hurried to Germany early in 1933 after the Nazis had occupied the Society's Bethel Home and printing plant at Magdeburg, about 50 miles from Berlin. The Nazis returned the property for a few months but again confiscated Witness headquarters in June. The 180 residents in Bethel were dispersed.

Hitler branded the Earnest Bible Students, as the Witnesses were generally known, as "troublemakers" and "quacks." Since title to the Watchtower plant was held by an American corporation, the State Department was able to negotiate the return of the property. The Nazis continued to enforce their ban on missionary activities, open meetings, and distribution of tracts.

As the Third Reich girded for war, persecution of the Bible Students intensified. Nazi orators demanded that all Bible Students be dismissed from their jobs. The Witnesses infuriated the new regime because they not only refused to vote or serve in the armed forces but even balked at giving the Hitler salute or joining in the Nazi-pagan celebrations. The Gestapo swooped down on observances of the Lord's Evening Meal in 1935 and arrested participants for defying the state's ban on such meetings.

In June 1937 the Reich Minister of Interior ordered that all Jehovah's Witnesses be turned over to the Gestapo. By the fall of that year the gates at Buchenwald had closed shut on 270 Witnesses; the Buchenwald congregation would reach more than 450 by the end of the year.

Between 1933 and 1945 the Nazis imprisoned about half the known German Witnesses at any given time. Those outside of the prisons and concentration camps met secretly, passed around mimeographed booklets, and gathered for occasional funerals.

Those who landed in the camps suffered a fate not much happier than that of the Jews. Camp officers first tried to induce the Witnesses to abjure their faith. They probably thought that since most of the Witnesses were Aryans they could be persuaded to abandon their peculiar religious views and taboos and rejoin the productive working force of the Third Reich. They offered them the opportunity to sign the following statement and leave the filthy camps for their homes as free men:

> I recognize that the International Society of Bible Students spreads out a doctrine of error, pursuing aims dangerous to the state, hidden behind religious actions.
>
> I therefore turned totally from this organization and freed myself completely from their doctrine.
>
> I assure by this never again to be active for the International Bible Students Society.
>
> I promise to deliver immediately every person communicating

this doctrine of error in my presence or showing a tendency as a Bible Student in some other way. I shall bring all Scriptures of the Bible Students handed over to me to the nearest office of police.

In future times I shall respect all the laws of the state to be completely a member of the community of the people.

I, too, have been taught to expect my repeated arrest, in case of violating my declaration given today.

Hardly any signed or recanted. The Witness inmates—called sky comedians and Bible worms by their SS tormentors—were beaten, tortured, stripped, and murdered. After the war broke out, the Witnesses at Sachsenhausen concentration camp were asked to volunteer for military service. When they refused, the SS picked ten men from their ranks and shot them. Four such refusals led to the death of 40 men before the SS gave up.

Late in 1941 the SS decided to launch a drive to collect woolens from the concentration camp inmates to send to the German armies on the eastern front. The camps seemed an unlikely place to find spare clothing but the 12,000 prisoners at Buchenwald contributed a small mountain of woolens. Only the Dutch prisoners and the Jehovah's Witnesses refused.

On New Year's Day, 1942, the SS commander ordered all Witnesses to fall in outside their barracks. "You archcriminals, you heavenly dogs, you'll slave tonight until dark at four degrees below! Take off your underwear at once!" They did. They were also forced to trade their leather shoes for wooden clogs. As part of the reprisal the SS removed Witnesses from their preferred jobs around the camp but soon reinstated them when they discovered the obedient orderlies and office workers were indispensable to camp operation.

A German author writes: "One cannot escape the impression that, psychologically speaking, the SS was never quite equal to the challenge offered them by Jehovah's Witnesses. They did not take the Witnesses altogether seriously, but rather had their cruel sport with them—a sort of cat-and-mouse game." [1]

Even in the camps the Witnesses continued to try to seek converts from their fellow prisoners. They used a water barrel for their baptisms. Miss Geneviève de Gaulle, a niece of the General, wrote: "They could have been immediately freed if they had renounced their faith. But on the contrary, they did not cease resistance, even succeeding in introducing books and tracts into the camp, which writings caused several among them to be hanged."

The Swedish journalist Bjorn Hallstrom observes simply: "They were treated worse than any other group, but they managed, through their belief in God, to survive better than any others."

Since the fall of the Third Reich in a Götterdämmerung of Soviet artillery and Allied blockbusters, the Witnesses have enjoyed a measure of prestige as one of the few elements of the nation to have resisted Nazism from the start. The utter destruction of many German cities and the horrors of the last days of the war prepared a good many Germans to listen to the warnings of Armageddon's imminence.

During the past two years the Witnesses have built 92 new Kingdom Halls. Ninety men and women live at Bethel in Wiesbaden and help supervise the 882 congregations in West Germany.

But as the West German economy staged its remarkable recovery and as the West Germans and even the West Berliners have learned to live with the daily threat of Communist attack, the growth of the Witnesses has slowed its pace. The percentage increase of 4 per cent for the year 1961 reflects no great rush to join the survivors of the SS camps and their postwar converts.

While the Gestapo was rounding up Bible Students in Nazi Germany, English judges were sentencing Witnesses to prison terms for draft evasion. By the start of the war the Society counted about 12,000 adherents in the British Isles. Many lost their homes and about a dozen died during the battle of Britain. But even at the height of the hostilities in September 1941, thousands of British Witnesses gathered at Leicester for a five-day convention to hear recordings by Judge Rutherford airmailed from Brooklyn.

The Society had opened its first branch office outside of the United States in England in 1900. In order to hold title to British property the Russellites organized under the name of the International Bible Students Association in 1914.

During World War II, most English judges refused to allow military exemptions to employed Witnesses: 1,593 convictions were meted out with prison sentences totaling more than 600 years. The government also forbade the importation of Watchtower publications. Elsewhere in the British Commonwealth the Society was either banned for a time, as in Canada and Australia, or restricted in its activities.

Today the New World Society claims more than 45,000 members in the British Isles, with a couple of hundred more in predominantly Catholic Ireland. Witnesses in England now outnumber such other sects as the Quakers, Unitarians, Mormons and Seventh-day Adventists. Mats of the *Watchtower* and *Awake!* magazines are flown from Brooklyn and printed on presses at the British Bethel in Mill Hill in northwest London. Local congregational servants are now attending four-week courses in a Kingdom Ministry School to prepare themselves better to fulfill their duties. There are 924 congregations.

Elsewhere on the continent the most promising field for the Society seems to be France. The average of 15,655 publishers in 1961 represents a 10 per cent increase over the previous year. Only three French cities with over 20,000 population remain untouched by Witness missionary efforts. The French branch recently dedicated a new Bethel and publishing house. It also supervises the work in French-speaking territories such as Algeria, Cameroun Republic, Republic of Guinea, Tunisia and Senegal.

In some European countries such as Denmark and Ireland the Society has actually lost members in recent years and in others the increase of brethren has been nominal. Recently the Witnesses won a court case in Belgium establishing the sect as a religion and Kingdom Halls as places of worship; this action meant that the Society could enjoy tax exemption. The *Yearbook* reports over 6,000 members in Belgium. The 1961 edition includes the story of the conversion of a young novice in a Catholic convent. Her brother and an interested streetcar conductor introduced her to Watchtower doctrines. The *Watchtower* for May 22, 1961, admits that "there is ample freedom in Italy for religious expression." The Italian Witnesses claim a membership of 5,838 for an 8 per cent boost over the previous year.

The Spanish government allows freedom of worship but forbids the kind of proselytizing by non-Catholic churches in which the Witnesses specialize. A Witness in Spain violates the law when he goes from door to door, advertises a public meeting, or tries to sell his publications on the street

Nevertheless, the number of Witnesses has grown from 121 ten years ago to a reported 2,141 in 1961.

Africa has become one of the Society's more fruitful fields. Recent statistics show five times as many Jehovah's Witnesses in Northern Rhodesia as in Italy and four times as many in Nigeria as in Greece. Work began in the early part of the century in South Africa and moved northward into British West Africa in the 1920's. Missionary activities also began in Egypt in the 1930's and spread across northern Africa.

The first group of 20 Gilead missionaries was dispatched to Africa in 1947 and hundreds have followed. Expansion in an area such as Northern Rhodesia has been so great that today we find that one out of 82 inhabitants calls himself a Witness of Jehovah, the highest ratio of Witnesses in any major area. Africans recognize the policy of strict racial equality in the Watchtower Society and realize that the Society owes no political obligations to the former colonial powers. The number of African Witnesses has jumped tenfold since 1942.

In order to work primarily through the printed word in these nations, the Society must often teach its prospective converts to read. It cooperates with a number of African governments in teaching natives the 3 R's. The text is called the *Theocratic Reader*. Kingdom Halls have become elementary schools as well as places of worship and religious instruction.

All-Witness villages in Africa are not uncommon. Like a Kingdom Hall or Witness assembly, they are characterized by tidiness and order. The villagers pay particular attention to sanitation, community gardens, roads, sexual conduct. Nevertheless *Life* magazine looked on Witness missions with some apprehension: "Of U. S. missions in Africa, not the least influential are Jehovah's Witnesses, whose gospel, so far as encouraging 'civilization,' abets the African's worst daydreams."

In Latin America the Watchtower Society plays upon the latent anticlericalism of the masses, nominally Roman Catholic. In 1942 the Witnesses counted only 807 publishers in all South America but in the 1962 *Yearbook* it reported 21,806 in Brazil, 7,672 in Argentina, 2,380 in Chile, and thousands of others in practically every Latin nation. More than 22,000 Mexicans have joined the sect and almost 13,000 Cuban Witnesses continue to practice their religion without interference by Castro.

Like many Protestant denominations, the Society shifted missionary emphasis from Asia and the Pacific Islands to Latin America during World War II. The first Gilead class learned conversational Spanish and beginning in 1943, graduates were sent to Cuba, Puerto Rico, Dominican Republic, Haiti, Trinidad, Bermuda, Jamaica and other Caribbean islands.

Sporadic witnessing was carried on in Argentina and Brazil as early as the 1920's but not until 1945 was a concentrated evangelistic campaign mapped by Brooklyn stategists. Results were gratifying. Gilead missionaries and native publishers attacked the mixture of paganism and Roman Catholicism which claims the allegiance of thousands in such countries as Haiti and Cuba. With tracts and pamphlets, sound trucks, and open-air meetings they ridiculed the veneration of the Virgin Mary, denounced the use of images in Catholic churches as idolatry, tried to sell Bibles and organize congregations. With millions of Latin Americans uninstructed in their Catholicism and constituting a typical proletarian group to which a proletarian message would make an immediate appeal, the Society found it difficult to ensure adequate indoctrination of its flood of converts.

To spite the Catholic hierarchy the late Dictator Trujillo lifted the ban against the Society in the Dominican Republic in 1960. In fact, the strong man invited the Society to resume sending missionaries to his island domain. Before this reprieve the Witnesses were forbidden to receive the *Watchtower* or other communication from Brooklyn. They could not form a branch or proselytize. Even with government encouragement, the Society reported only 617 members in 1961 out of a population of nearly 3,000,000.

On the other hand, the Watchtower boasted a 17 per cent increase in the largest South American nation: Brazil. In 1940 the peak number of publishers was only 248. In 1960 more than 27,000 Brazilians attended the 17 district assemblies held in various sections of the huge country.

North of the border in Canada the Watchtower enjoys a more favorable ratio of members to total population than in the United States itself. The Society's activities were banned by the Canadian government during both World Wars but Witnesses now number 36,459, or one in 465 Canadians. A total of 58,000 attended the Memorial Meal, which indicates that at least 20,000 more consider Kingdom Hall their spiritual home. As in the United States, the Society in Canada has won a series of court cases establishing its right to seek converts. It seems to concentrate on the French-speaking Catholic population in Quebec but has its strongholds in British Columbia and Saskatchewan.

Considerable success has been recorded in another predominantly Catholic nation, the Philippines. Peak number of publishers in 1961 was 35,713; there were only 2,000 Witnesses there in 1945. Many if not most of these converts were former Roman Catholics, although the Witnesses also try to win Seventh-day Adventists, Protestants, and Aglipayans.

Outside of Africa, the Witnesses seem to register their best gains in countries at least nominally Christian. Unless a prospective convert already believes in God and in the inspiration of the Bible the Witness missionary faces a difficult task establishing his apologetical credentials.

Again and again in reports from overseas missionaries of the New World Society, the story is told of how a Catholic priest or nun, a Protestant minister, or a church elder encounters a dedicated Witness who confounds him by his command of Bible truths and godly wisdom. Readers of the *Yearbook* hear about elderly priests who get their first opportunity to see a Bible when shown one by a young Gilead graduate. After a few study sessions, we are told, the Catholic tears off his religious habit, burns his rosary and smashes his statues, and sets about devouring the word of Jehovah God.

Anyone familiar with the religious situation in Latin countries needs no one to tell him that most of the people must be considered nominal or lax Catholics by Church standards of Mass attendance, fasting, marriage laws, etc. That Gilead products with a high school education and a short course in Bible can best very many clergymen in theological debate is another matter and may represent a wish fulfillment rather than a strictly accurate journalistic account.

Behind the Iron Curtain the various Communist governments have banned the Society as a reactionary American tool. Nevertheless the 1962 *Yearbook* reported an average of 114,161 publishers in ten Red nations, a decrease of more than 7 per cent under the preceding year.

As in Nazi Germany, the Communists have sentenced hundreds of Witnesses to prisons and Siberian labor camps. Especially in Poland and the USSR, the authorities have planted spies in local congregations to expose the membership and discover how they manage to carry on underground literature dissemination. The Society, however, claims that ten such spies have left the Communist Party to join the New World Society.

Pravda attacked the Society in 1959: "From the very first day of its existence the sect called Jehovah's Witnesses entered the service of the most reactionary circles of American capital. Wealthy patrons gave the new sect entry into the colonial countries to implant a spirit of mute submissiveness and set the Witnesses on the young socialist movement in Europe. In our time these patrons are trying to use them as a subversive force in the socialist countries" (March 18, 1959).

In this *Pravda* article, entitled "Apostles of the Powder Keg," the writer revealed that Witnesses were becoming more active in the Kurgan, Irkutsk and Tomsk provinces and the Western Ukraine. The police discovered mimeograph machines, phonograph records and tracts. The Red reporter concludes: "One cannot remain indifferent to indications that this dark force is becoming more active."

The 1961 *Yearbook* states: "Jehovah's Witnesses continue to take a neutral position in the Communist countries, as they have done all over the world, having nothing to do with politics" (p. 275). In this sense Communist persecution of the Witnesses, or Jehovists as they are called, differs from that of the Catholics. Communists know that the Church opposes atheistic Communism as a materialistic philosophy and forbids the faithful to support or vote for Communist candidates in the West. The Witnesses of Jehovah vote for no political party, take no interest in politics, castigate capitalism and democracy as much as Communism and fascism. A plague on both your Satanic political affairs, say the Witnesses.

Some 468 Witnesses languish in East German prisons and during 1960 alone, 97 were arrested. Some of the first Witnesses sentenced in 1950 to ten-year terms were finally released. Two Witnesses have been given life terms and 33 others must serve from 12 to 15 years.

During a trial of Witnesses in Poland the prosecuting attorney declared, "The program of governmental politics includes the liquidation of all religions, because they are unscientific. But the worst of them all is the religion of Jehovah's Witnesses, and we have to liquidate that one first." More than 300 Polish Witnesses were involved in court cases during the year and 180 of these received sentences amounting to 160 years and fines totaling 100,000 zlotys.

An antireligious exhibit in Lvov included an attack on the Witnesses. The newspaper *Vilna Ukraina* reported, "The exhibition also displays the activity of the highly reactionary sect of Jehovists in the territory of the Western Ukraine, the headquarters of which group is located in Brooklyn, U.S.A." (Nov. 24, 1959). The Party line brands the Watchtower as a "political underground organization" which is "carrying on destructive, subversive activity against the Soviet government, publicly propagating a new war." Apparently this new war is Armageddon. The Soviets have even produced a film about the sect called *Apostles Unmasked* which has been shown in many cities and villages. *Pravda* insists that the Witness organizers are "former war criminals, fascist collaborators and Gestapo informers" who were trained in Nazi concentration camps. Certainly many were trained in concentration camps, not by the Gestapo but by fellow Bible students.

Dr. George N. Shuster, then president of Hunter College, analyzed Communist persecution of Jehovah's Witnesses, in his study of religion in Russia and the satellite nations.

> The full weight of Communist opposition fell on Jehovah's Witnesses, a sect which has long had a following in Eastern Europe and so was well known in some sections of the expellee population. The Witnesses had also been a target for Nazi hostility, and many hundreds of them perished in Dachau and other concentration camps. During 1950, the Communists banned the sect in eastern Germany, on the ground that it was a branch of the American "espionage system," even though specially favorable treatment had been accorded it in Poland. It is believed that by the close of the year nearly 800 Witnesses were serving terms in prison and in labor camps, and that life sentences had been imposed on 13 of its principal advocates.
>
> Jehovah's Witnesses believe that the end of the world is rapidly approaching, on the basis of their deductions from Holy Writ, and therefore indulge in prophecies concerning the impending demise of our world, due to sin and frailty. Communism believes in prophecy, too, but holds that the sole reliable form of soothsaying is that outlined by Marxist philosophy as a corollary of "natural science." This "science" enabled Stalin to predict the future of human society with complete accuracy. Communist literature is therefore rich in attacks on "bourgeois" and "mystical" soothsayers, and in equally savory eulogies of Stalin as a social-scientific fortune teller. But Jehovah's Witnesses, confident that the Word of God had been vouchsafed for them, are incorrigible. No "patriots" or "democrats" have ever been reported from their ranks.[2]

Delegates to a Witness district assembly in North Carolina in 1956 addressed a petition to the Soviet premier pointing out: "They [Jehovah's Witnesses] remain neutral toward the controversies of this world. So they do not engage in any subversive activity and espionage. They are not nationalists, selfish capitalists or imperialists." To further appease the Red ruler the petition noted, "They are intelligent people who do not believe in all the oppression and misinstruction by false religions. They do not steal, they do not get drunk and thus slow down production, and they will never engage in any sabotage work." In other words, despite persecution by the Communists the Witnesses cannot be considered allies or sympathizers of the free world either.

As usual the Witnesses produce a prophetic explanation for their difficulties behind the Iron Curtain. "God's prophetic Word, according to the book of Daniel, shows that the present-day prophetic 'king of the north' is the ruling factor of world communism and that this Communist 'king' will eventually launch a full-scale attack against Jehovah's witnesses."[3] This attack against the Witnesses will eventually take precedence over the Communist campaign against the "king of the south," meaning the "Anglo-American world power."

In Tito's Yugoslavia the Witnesses are legally recognized and relatively free to preach and distribute tracts and books. Two Witnesses were imprisoned in Shanghai in 1958 and have not been released despite the best efforts of the Society. Actually the Watchtower had not engaged in extensive missionary work in China before the Red take-over. In other Asian nations such as India and Japan membership is small.

Although the Pastor and the Judge had tried to establish the Society on a world-wide basis, it was not until Knorr's administration that the practical steps to achieve this goal were taken. Chief among these was the founding of the Watchtower Bible School of Gilead.

Since 1935 the Society had operated an 800-acre farm about 250 miles northwest of New York City and nine miles north of Ithaca. In 1942 the board of directors decided to open a missionary Bible school there.

Four veteran Witnesses prepared the course of study, collected a basic library of 1,400 books, chose suitable textbooks among those issued by the Society or, in the case of language and speech texts, by secular publishers. They designed a 5½-month program to accommodate 100 students at a time. The students would be brought to the school, housed and fed by the Society. The first class, all Americans because of wartime travel restrictions, enrolled in January 1943.

Only pioneers with at least two years of experience were eligible to register. The course covered such subjects as Bible, public speaking, arithmetic, English, international law, and foreign languages. After completing the course graduates agreed to accept any assignment the Society made. The first class specialized in Spanish, since it was impractical to think of sending missionaries anywhere but to Latin America at that time.

The Gilead student body, ranging in age from twenty to fifty-nine and including married couples, spent the morning and early afternoon hours in class. At 2:30 all students began their daily three hours of farm or household chores.

After the war, applications from outside the United States were accepted and eventually more than half the student body was composed of foreign students. All needed a working knowledge of English before starting the course.

Depending on the current missionary objectives, the school taught one particular foreign language to each class: Spanish, French, Italian, Japanese, Arabic, Portuguese, Urdu and Malayan. On Sundays the students would scatter to 20 congregations within a 60-mile radius of the campus to put in their door-to-door preaching hours.

Like Bethel residents the faculty and farm managers got only room, board and $14 a month. Nobody smoked and all worked in some capacity.

Eventually the school added a new library building with 10,000 volumes and an observatory with a 16-inch reflector-type telescope. Ten years after its founding Gilead received the approval of the U. S. Office of Education, which enabled the school to enroll foreign students under the nonimmigrant student visa arrangement.

Jehovah's Witnesses display a touching pride in their little school. "Gilead is not the largest school in the world, nor the most celebrated, but it is without question the best. . . . No other school can boast of so many graduates producing good fruit to the honor of God's name. As an educator in scriptural truth it stands alone among the schools of the world." So declared a Watchtower newsletter in 1958.

In 1960 the Society moved the school from South Lansing to Brooklyn. During the 17 years in upstate New York the school had registered 3,738 students, of whom 3,432 won their diplomas. They came from 95 different countries and were sent to more than 100 countries as full-time missionaries. School records indicate that about 8 out of 100 of the students professed to be among the 13,000 of the remnant while the rest were content to be "other sheep." Facilities at the former campus have been turned over to the Kingdom Ministry School to train 100 congregational overseers every month.

Gilead graduates form the nucleus of the Society's global missionary program. They were not sent to these countries to take over or supervise Watchtower affairs although some have since become branch, district and circuit servants. The

Society provides housing, medical care, clothing allowance, transportation and food. A fledgling Gilead missionary spends the first month studying the language for 11 hours a day. During his second month he spends four hours in language practice and the rest of the day in preaching activities. After this he is expected to devote at least two hours a day on language until he masters the native tongue. Once established, he should spend 150 hours a month or more in his ministry work.

The Society keeps a close tab on these missionaries. In an article on marriage and the moral standards in some foreign countries, the *Watchtower* warns: "This is something for missionary girls to think of seriously in their foreign assignments, when they are ardently pursued by smoothly operating native boys and men who put on a front of interest in the Bible message borne by the missionary girl and then try them out with improper suggestive advances, to soften them up." [4]

These Watchtower missionaries, unlike Catholic and Protestant missionaries, confine their activities to strictly religious work. The Society explains, "The Christian [Jehovah's Witnesses] missionary's errand is not an economic aid program to various backward countries or handicapped lands. Ours is the more vital religious aid program." A Watchtower missionary who began to spend time teaching agricultural methods or healing the sick could expect a sharp reprimand from Brooklyn.

Formal organization of the Society's missionary program and the setting up of the short course at Gilead sparked much of the amazing membership increase during the past two decades. Certainly the Society could not have enjoyed a 2,000 per cent growth in a country such as Panama in a scant 15 years without Gilead and full-time personnel.

During 1961 the Society operated in 185 nations, islands and protectorates through 85 branch offices. A total of 884,587 ment and women considered ordained ministers helped gather 33,209 additional Witnesses for an over-all membership gain of 3.9 per cent. The 1961 gain in 175 areas outside of the Iron Curtain was 42,614 Witnesses for a 5.8 per cent increase but this was offset by losses in Communist-controlled countries. As many as 956,169 publishers distributed Watchtower books and magazines and more than 1,550,000 attended the Lord's Evening Meal in 1961.

Considering the notorious unreliability of religious statistics, the outsider may stifle a smile when he reads in the official 1961 *Yearbook*: "In fact, during the year they [Jehovah's Witnesses] discussed the Bible truths with the people of the world for 131,662,684 hours. This is 5,345,560 more hours than they spent in the preaching work during the previous year." No round numbers for Watchtower statisticians.

The Society designated 6,377 men and women as special pioneers in 1961 who were sent to isolated areas to labor as missionaries. Another 23,467 regular pioneers put in an average of 100 hours a month working with local established congregations. Special pioneers were supposed to log at least 150 hours a month. To support these missionaries the Society spent more than $2,300,000 in 1961. This comes from donations by Witnesses and any profits from the publishing business.

The Knorr administration no doubt sees its greatest potential for growth in South America and Africa. It has hardly enough converts in Japan and India to organize its work and cannot get into Red China. And even the Witnesses' dreadful picture of Armageddon would probably not faze the man on the streets of Hiroshima and Nagasaki.

Witnesses obviously exult in the spread of the Society around the world and like to point out that every 82nd citizen of Northern Rhodesia has already cast his lot with the New World Society. At the same time, the most recent Yearbook indicates that the ratio of Witnesses to non-Witnesses in Afghanistan is 1 to 1,200,000. This and similar lopsided ratios in many countries present a challenge to the indefatigable Gilead graduate and pioneer.

10. *Attitudes Toward Church and State*

Sociologists of religion distinguish the sect from the church by their respective attitudes toward the state and the established church. This distinction will help us understand Jehovah's Witnesses as well.

At least in its early years the sect counsels its members to steer clear of the state and all its works and pomps. The infant sect often preaches pacifism, abstention from politics, and refusal to acknowledge the symbols of the state such as the national flag or obedience to the king or sovereign.

To the original sectaries the state represents the entrenched wicked order. It deserves no allegiance, especially by true reborn Christians. Drawing most of its adherents from the "out" classes of society, the proletariat, the sect finds it relatively easy to urge its members to take the final step and disavow any interest at all in secular affairs. Chances are these folks wield little influence in the halls of government and commerce anyway.

Over the years this typically sectarian posture toward the state may mellow. Today the spiritual descendants of the

Anabaptists—the Mennonites—still object to military service but raise no objection to voting, participating in local and national politics, pledging allegiance and saluting the flag. Quakers have abandoned their quiet protests against the use of titles and honorific forms of address; a Quaker who joins the army during war no longer jeopardizes his standing in the Friends community. President Herbert Hoover, a Quaker, served as commander in chief of the armed forces and another Quaker, Richard Nixon, wanted to try his hand at the same job.

Occasionally a faction will protest against such accommodation to the ways of the world. It may try to reform the parent body as did the strict Amish Mennonites. The result is usually a schism.

Just as the sect passes a negative judgment against the state, so it excoriates the practices of the established church. To the sect the church must be a body of regenerated saints and not a conglomeration of saints and sinners. The sect insists that the Christian church admit to membership only adult believers who undergo baptism by immersion. Furthermore, the sect vigorously culls the sinners and backslidden from its ranks and employs systems of excommunication and disfellowshiping. The Mennonites punish those who leave the straight and narrow by shunning, a sort of silent treatment whereby nobody, not even the victim's family, speaks or acknowledges the excommunicated one's existence.

The church in contrast assumes that all or most members of the nation will be baptized into its fellowship in infancy. Rarely do individuals incur public excommunication. In maturity the church displays a degree of tolerance toward human weaknesses and foibles which scandalizes the sects.

Whether Catholic or Protestant, the church becomes an

object of scorn to the sectarians. Full of nominal Christians, the churches have betrayed the pure faith once delivered to the saints, say the sects. They have allowed doctrinal errors, paganism, license, worldly values, to creep into the Christian life. And they are beyond reform; only a complete break with these apostate churches will remedy the situation and restore primitive Christianity.

Usually the huge and ancient Roman Catholic Church bears the brunt of the sects' denunciations. She becomes the whore of Babylon, the scarlet woman, the anti-Christ. The sects might admit that a few genuine Christians can be discovered even in the Roman communion but the system itself stands condemned as the instrument of Satan. Protestant denominations such as Lutheranism and Anglicanism failed to root out all the evils of Romanism at the time of the Reformation and remain infected by many of the errors of Rome. They too seek and enjoy the patronage of the state and stand condemned.

Again, over the decades the sects may alter their original positions. We might compare this change of heart or softening with the change in a politician who finally wins the office for which he has been campaigning and comes now to know firsthand some of the knotty problems his opponent, the incumbent, has faced. The harsh and bitter charges he once leveled in the heat of the campaign fade into the background as the winner finds he has his hands full meeting these same problems and dealing with the same human characteristics and limited by many of the same restrictions.

Many sects have long ago modified their views of fellow Protestants even though they may continue to look upon Catholicism with a good deal of lingering suspicion. The sect-turned-church may eventually join national and world associations of churches, cooperate in community ministerial alliances, train ministers in interdenominational seminaries, cultivate ecumenical relations. All these actions would have filled their grandparents with horror and dismay.

In other areas the sect compromises and softens its stand. In its infancy the sect probably looked on seminary training and higher education in general as a contributing factor to pride and theological obscurity. After all, the apostles and Jesus Himself attended no such school. But as the years pass, the sect may find it desirable to set up liberal arts colleges for its young people. Then the larger, more affluent congregations begin to ask for ministers with college degrees and formal training. The clergy themselves realize that without such training their advancement is uncertain and the most sought-after pulpits are closed. Before the cycle ends, the sect's leading congregations expect their pastors to wear Ph.D. hoods or sign their names with the D.D. designation.

Liturgically the sect starts out with the plainest ritual. One of the objections to Rome is her use of images, incense, vestments, stained glass, which appeal to man's lower, i.e. sensual, appetites. Members of the sect meet in bare, whitewashed meetinghouses to hear the Bible read, offer extemporaneous prayers, and sing simple hymns or the Psalms. Art is outlawed. Today the visitor to the church of sectarian beginnings may find a pipe organ and trained choir, stained glass, pulpit robes for the minister, an altar where once stood the pulpit, possibly candles and flowers, few spontaneous prayers.

Sociologists indicate that this progression from sect to church follows a pattern which seldom varies. Many sects have now reached church status; some sects are passing through the transformation before our eyes. Sometimes the change takes hundreds of years, sometimes a few decades.

In a real sense the sects themselves hasten the process by their influence on their members. The sects urge hard work, total abstinence, simple living. These habits of life in turn should result in greater affluence. Members move from unskilled to white-collar jobs, their children begin to seek college educations, their tastes improve and they begin to wonder why their church limits itself to swingy gospel tunes instead of Bach and Palestrina. Eventually the middle-class members either help transform the sect into a church or abandon the lagging sect for a church home more suited to their new social and economic status.

Jehovah's Witnesses reveal most of the characteristics of the sect in its early stages. Founded as a formal religious body in 1884 the Watchtower Society would be considered a youngster among the sects but already we can observe several significant modifications of the sectarian impulse.

For example, the typically sectarian congregational polity gave way in 1938 to a highly centralized form of church government. Certain Puritan attitudes against the use of liquor and tobacco persist but the Watchtower Society refuses to make total abstinence a test of fellowship. Pastor Russell scorned all formal theological education but the Society set up a program of resident instruction at the Watchtower Bible School of Gilead in 1944; the original 5½-month Gilead course has recently been stretched to ten months. Except for local pastors (congregational overseers), the Watchtower has come to rely more and more on full-time, trained personnel for overseas missionary work and supervision.

Nevertheless, the sectarian protest against society and society's institutions can be seen clearly in the Watchtower

Bible and Tract Society. Only the tiny Amish communities, the Black Muslims, and the cults of Southern California compare in these attempts to isolate adherents from the mainstream of American society.

The Watchtower Society has developed a theory of noninvolvement in the affairs of the secular state based on the recognized rights of aliens. Philip Nolan becomes their hero. Jehovah's Witnesses are told again and again that they must become men without a country. Since all worldly governments serve Satan and his cohorts, the Witnesses of Jehovah should feel under no obligation to render these governments any allegiance. All governments—democratic, Communist, socialist, fascist, monarchist—refuse to acknowledge Jehovah's theocracy as revealed by the Watchtower Society and all without exception will go down at Armageddon.

The Society instructs its members that they have become ministers or ambassadors of the kingdom of Jesus Christ through their baptism of dedication. "It follows that its members or ambassadors deserve the same rights and exemptions as such officials of this world enjoy." [1]

The Society's basic doctrinal exposition further explains:

> An ambassador of a foreign power is by the laws of this world exempted as an alien from giving allegiance to the government of the land in which he is resident. He is relieved of rendering political obligations of any sort. The nation where he resides is without authority to impose any regulation that burdens or abridges his performing duty as such.[2]

> Since Jehovah has chosen his witnesses out of the world to be ambassadors in behalf of his kingdom to the peoples of the earth, they are no part of this world. As their allegiance is to

the Most High God and his kingdom, they do not take part in local, national or international elections or politics.[3]

Witnesses will appeal to the courts of the land to protect their rights and will pay whatever taxes may be levied, but so will any alien. They refuse to render to Caesar that which is Caesar's since Caesar is simply Satan in disguise. If Caesar were a legitimate ruler he would recognize the theocratic rule of the Watchtower Bible and Tract Society of 124 Columbia Heights, Brooklyn, New York. He would also stop persecuting Jehovah's Witnesses.

Today the United Nations in particular comes in for scathing criticism in Watchtower books, periodicals and lectures as did its predecessor, the League of Nations. These international bodies seek to guarantee world peace in defiance of Jehovah's determination to destroy all worldly states in the coming Götterdämmerung of Armageddon. *Let God Be True* explains: "His [Satan's] devices for fooling people appear very innocent. A United Nations and other world security organizations, united church movements, and the like, are all his schemes to blind people to the real remedy." [4]

Seldom will a Witness speaker miss the opportunity to blast the UN and ridicule its inability to settle international conflicts. Whenever the UN fails, the Watchtower gloats that Satan's devious ways have once again been frustrated. The patient is not supposed to get well but get progressively worse until he faces the crisis hour of Armageddon.

In an exercise in simplified history the Society explains the failure of the earlier League of Nations: "The pope was excluded from a seat in the League, and so the Roman Catholic Hierarchy set out to destroy it by Fascism and Nazism. This she accomplished through totalitarian aggressors, and the League bowed from the scene during World War II, into the abyss." [5] In two sentences the Watchtower historian can describe the demise of the hated League of Nations by means of the machinations of the equally hated Catholic hierarchy.

Denying that the creation of the state of Israel conforms to the biblical prophecy of the return of the Jews to their homeland, the Society generally attacks Zionism. Recognition of the new state by the United States and later the United Nations confirms the Watchtower's view of the essential wickedness of the Jewish state.

Since Russell's time the Watchtower Society has branded orthodox Christianity as hypocritical, pagan, corrupt, venal and Satanic. The Pastor maintained that during the past 1,300 years the Papacy directly or indirectly had murdered 50,000,000 people.[6]

He thought little more of Anglicanism and indicated in the preface to his *The Battle of Armageddon* that the Church of England was represented in the Bible by the two-horned beast.

> Thus the Church in England, casting aside some of the grosser doctrines and practices of the Church of Rome, claimed and still claims, that it is the only true Church, and that its bishops have apostolic succession, and hence supreme control of God's heritage.[7]

He repeats the same charge in a later volume:

> The Church of England makes the claim which the Church of Rome makes—that she is the true Church; that all others are wrong; that she has the original apostolic succession; and that no one is commissioned to preach unless he has had the divine, apostolic hands laid upon him.[8]

Judge Rutherford intensified Russell's attacks on the traditional churches and urged his followers to throw caution to the wind. Witnesses during the 1930's paraded before churches with signs calling religion a racket and a snare. Caricatures of priests, Popes and Protestant ministers filled the pages of Watchtower books, magazines and tracts. President Knorr has toned down some of the tactics but his complete opposition to Christendom remains.

The Catholic and Protestant churches of Christendom are not merely mistaken in their theology; they are part of Satan's worldly apparatus. A book which appeared two years after the start of Knorr's administration said: "Babylon on earth became the nursing place of organized religion which is demonism or demonolatry." [9] The same volume referred to the "devilish racket of religion" and charges: "Religion is the adultress and idolatress that befriends and commits religious fornication with the political and commercial elements. She is the lover of this world and blesses the world from the balcony of the Vatican and in the pulpits." [10]

In a later book one of the Society's anonymous authors writes: "Logically, God hates Christendom. Soon he will destroy her with the rest of the world." [11] Repeating the theme of an unholy alliance, the same book declares: "Contrary to its Christian claims, Christendom is wicked in its disobedience to God and is adulterous in its unclean friendly connections with the political and commercial elements of this world." [12]

These sample passages lump together the three elements of the hated triumvirate: church, state and business. The first two receive most of the Watchtower anathemas but the third element—the business and commercial world—will also get its just due at Armageddon. To discover a faithful Witness who was a stockbroker or corporation lawyer would be like finding a Methodist running a distillery or a Roman Catholic a contraceptive factory.

Catholicism comes in for a greater share of Watchtower invective but Protestantism and to some extent Judaism also get some attention. Witnesses believe that the Reformation never really got off the ground and that the Protestant reformers carried along too many "pagan" doctrines such as the Trinity, the divinity of Christ, immortality, etc. In *Jehovah's Witnesses in the Divine Purpose* we read:

> Many Protestant leaders were as vicious in their persecution of religious opponents as the Inquisition of the Catholic Church had been. For example, John Calvin had the anti-trinitarian Michael Servetus literally roasted alive, in horrible torture, for nearly five hours before he expired, while Calvin watched from a window. Furthermore, the Protestant churches carried over with them the same teachings of apostacy that had been believed during the centuries of papal rule. These facts alone are evidence that this was not a true Reformation, nor were these "Reformers" witnesses of Jehovah as Jesus and those before him had been.[13]

The manual for Witness ministers comments:

> The Reformation rather than being a restoration of true worship, essentially brought in a change in church government from hierarchic to that of episcopal and congregational. The original theocratic form of the early church was not restored. Contrary to what is generally thought, the Reformation did not bring in a large number of reforms as to fundamental church doctrines, which continued to be heavily tainted with paganism.[14]

According to Witness historians, the Roman Catholic Church started in the fourth century and the Emperor

Constantine was the first Pope. "Constantine was really the first Roman Catholic pope." [15]

A special edition of *Awake!* on October 8, 1960, discussed the role of the Catholic Church in modern life. "That the major blame for World War II must be laid at the feet of totalitarianism, and especially Nazism, is well known. But not equally well known is that fact that the Roman Catholic Church played the leading role in Nazifying Germany." [16] The Witness commentators identify Hitler, Goebbels and Mussolini as obedient Catholics and add: "The great majority of the Nazi hierarchy were Roman Catholics even though Germany at the time was only about one third Roman Catholic." [17]

On page 24 of this issue an article entitled "The Catholic Church and Morals" is illustrated by a drawing of a cassocked priest eying a shapely young girl in the best Maria Monk tradition. To buttress its claim that Catholicism promotes immorality, the magazine refers to a case of alleged drunkenness among the clergy of Chicago in 1902. It quotes Machiavelli, who is identified as a "Catholic statesman and political writer": "We Italians are indebted principally to the Church and the priests for having become impious and immoral." Machiavelli's *The Prince* is listed on the Index of Forbidden Books and therefore forbidden to Catholic readers except with special permission. A news item quotes an ex-priest, Peter J. Doeswyck, as declaring in a speech at East Lansing, Michigan, that while in training for the priesthood he had never read the Bible. He did not identify the Catholic seminary which prepared him for the priesthood without requiring the usual Scripture courses. Finally the magazine brands the Catholic Church as immoral for not outlawing gambling.

Qualified to Be Ministers refers to the Roman Catholic Church in the following terms: "Upon these filthy, fourth-century fusion foundations Satan has erected his gigantic, lawless, anti-Christ organization, a masterpiece of deception, iniquity, and oppression all guided under the hierarchic priesthood after the order of Nimrod." [18]

A recent article in *Awake!* continues the crusade against the traditional churches: "Religious teachings such as Christmas and Easter, while widely popular among professed Christians, are still pagan and unchristian. . . . Doctrines that represent God as a freak and a fiend, such as trinity, purgatory, and a hell-fire where souls are tormented in flames for all eternity, will be vigorously challenged by Christians and exposed as being of demonic origin. Christians will not tolerate in silence such blasphemies against God, neither will they allow religious gambling, clerical hypocrisy, and religious warmongering to go unmentioned in the name of tolerance." [19]

Some Witnesses take the defensive when others ask why the New World Society supports no hospitals, colleges, orphanages, homes for the aged, or other charitable institutions. That Christian churches do engage in such eleemosynary activities only emphasizes their guilt, according to the Witnesses: "Christendom will yet hear these stinging words of condemnation unveiling her hypocrisy spoken to her at Armageddon. She loudly boasts of her charitable works, parades them before the public eye and takes up collections of millions of dollars, aside from the bingo gambling racket, to draw support of such charities from others. But it is a historical fact, undeniably backed up by the records in the courts of the law, that she has no charity for the remnant of Christ's brothers [the anointed among Jehovah's Witnesses], even the least of them." [20]

That many orthodox clergymen and scholars now admit the possibility of the evolution of the human body riles the Witnesses: "Many Catholic, Protestant and Jewish clergymen have embraced it [the theory of evolution], and thus accept this dogma of ancient pagans along with some of their other pagan doctrines, such as trinity and immortal soul and eternal torment." [21]

Witnesses sneer at the building of costly churches and synagogues although their own Kingdom Halls are becoming more elaborate every year. From rented store fronts many congregations have moved to their own Kingdom Hall buildings. Per member these halls may well cost as much as a Catholic parish serving not 100 or 200 individuals but as many as 1,000 families.

Witnesses continue to inveigh against religious holy days, seminaries, ecclesiastical titles, fasting, the Lenten season, the use of the cross as the Christian symbol, etc. No doubt such criticisms also help cement the *esprit de corps* of the New World Society. While the nation celebrates Christmas the Witness goes about his everyday business with a certain sense of superiority that he is not like other men. Unlike them he knows that this holy day–holiday is nothing but a pagan winter festival taken over by Christendom.

Again basing his stand on the doubtful translation of certain Greek words, the Witness corrects the nominal Christians of Christendom who think Jesus was crucified on a cross. Not at all, says the Witness. He was rather impaled on a torture stake which had no crossbeam. To imagine otherwise only exposes Christendom's pagan orientation. And yet both Russell and Rutherford made numerous references to the

Cross and the Crucifixion. In a book such as the Judge's *Creation* (1927) the Watchtower Society included two full-color reproductions of the Crucifixion for the edification of the readers. Nary a sign of the torture stake.

Another peculiarity of Witness art is the representation of Jesus without a beard. Most Christian artists today paint Jesus with a full beard and long hair. Here, however, the Witnesses may appeal to early Christian art which also presented a beardless Saviour.

Why hundreds of millions of people remain in the "apostate" churches of Christendom is explained by a Witness author: "The men who see the double-talk and double-dealing of the clergy have no use for these religious hypocrites. But because their womenfolk hold to the religious system, the men make no disturbance about it just in order to keep their women and get along with them."[22]

Almost every issue of *Watchtower* and *Awake!* reprints quotations by Protestant and Catholic writers which point up the weaknesses, ineffectuality and sins of the traditional churches. That such self-criticism might be a healthy sign never occurs to the editors. That similar soul-searching in official Watchtower publications is conspicuous by its absence is ignored. After all, the troubles that afflict Christendom's churches and sects should not plague Jehovah's own New World Society.

The Witnesses firmly believe they are the only people on the face of the globe who are faithfully doing the will of God. They belong to the only organization—religious or secular—to which Jehovah God has given his blessing. All other religions are false. The Christian churches deserve more condemnation because they falsely pose as the teaching representatives of Jesus Christ while actually serving Satan. And they will get theirs at Armageddon.

> Though all other kinds disagree with it, there must be only one kind of worship, one religion, that is right. This is the one in harmony with absolute truth. Since there is just the one that is true, set against so many hundreds of others that prove to be false, it follows that those who adopt and practice the true must necessarily be in the minority.[23]

By assiduously cultivating these attitudes of separation and criticism the Society weans its followers away from old thought patterns and associations. Witnesses live in a world of their own, one which they believe to be cleaner, far more righteous, than any other. They need assume no blame or responsibility for mankind's failures, wars and follies since they have renounced all worldly citizenship for citizenship and service in Jehovah's own Theocracy. This release from guilt may be just as effective as the couch and the confessional.

11. *Witnesses in Court*

TEST CASES which reach the Supreme Court serve as benchmarks in the attainment of civil rights. Much of the recent progress in the area of civil rights, outside of the racial decisions, was won in legal battles waged by Jehovah's Witnesses lawyers and their courtroom allies. In fact, in recent years the Society has taken 50 test cases to the Supreme Court and won 37 of them.

Especially between the years 1937 and 1946, the attempts to hamstring the proselytizing activities of the unpopular Witnesses and the sentiment of a nation at war toward what it considered to be cantankerous draft dodgers brought hundreds of cases to the dockets. We have seen how Judge Rutherford and his fellow Watchtower officers fared during the hysteria of World War I. Popular opinion against the larger, more visible and aggressive sect before and during World War II was even more widespread and bitter.

Hayden Covington, the Society's legal counsel after the Judge's death, described some of the hardships which many Witnesses endured during these years: "In 44 states they were beaten, kidnapped, tarred and feathered, throttled on castor oil, tied together and chased through the streets, castrated, maimed, hanged, shot, and otherwise consigned to mayhem."

Somehow the U. S. courts had to preserve the rights entailed in freedom of religion and speech while protecting also the rights of the general public against public nuisances, impromptu parades down Main Street, the blare of loudspeakers on a quiet Sunday afternoon. Local draft boards had to consider the claims of thousands of draft-age able-bodied young men who said they were "ministers" of Jehovah but held full-time jobs in defense industries. Later the courts would have to decide between the sacred rights of parents and the rights of a child to life when the parents for religious reasons refused to allow a blood transfusion which competent medical authorities considered necessary to preserve life.

A study of the Fund for the Republic states: "State legislation has frequently been aimed at or applied against Jehovah's Witnesses, and this sect has been responsible for making much of the law of religious freedom." [1]

A publication of the American Bar Association credits the Watchtower with strengthening the constitutional freedoms of all Americans by its multiple test cases.

> Seldom, if ever, in the past, has one individual or group been able to shape the course, over a period of time, of any phase of our vast body of constitutional law. But it can happen, and it has happened, here. The group is Jehovah's Witnesses. Through almost constant litigation this organization has made possible an ever-increasing list of precedents concerning the application of the Fourteenth Amendment to freedom of speech and religion. . . . The decisions resulting therefrom now set the pattern for state courts in determining how far state legislatures may validly proceed on matters pertaining to freedom of speech

and religion. The cases assume greater and greater significance, as local legislative bodies, with one type of law ruled unconstitutional, proceed to new and different devices aimed at curtailment. Thus, while the cult though vigorously active, has but negligible influence, its incidental contributions to constitutional law have been tremendously significant.[2]

The first Witness was arrested in 1928 for preaching on Sunday and the Society's early legal battles centered around the right to engage in door-to-door evangelism, street distribution of tracts, and other typical Witness techniques.

The city of Griffin, Georgia, enforced a municipal ordinance which forbade the distribution of literature without the written consent of the city manager. The Witnesses took the case to court and in 1938 the Supreme Court invalidated the ordinance as constituting prior censorship and thereby violating the First Amendment. The next year the court struck down four similar ordinances in New Jersey communities.

Yet in *Cox v. New Hampshire* (1941) the court held that Jehovah's Witnesses were limited just as were other groups in conducting parades. This meant that they had to obtain a license and pay any regulatory fee required by the city. The city authorities could also specify an hour for the parade when the public would not be unduly disturbed.

Later a Witness was convicted in Dallas, Texas, for passing out handbills on the city streets. The city maintained that this violated a city ordinance which prohibited the scattering of leaflets or handbills on public thoroughfares. Many people naturally discarded the Watchtower literature and the city fathers probably wanted to try to keep the streets clean. Nevertheless the Supreme Court supported the Society in

Jamison v. Texas (1943). ". . . [The states] may not prohibit the distribution of handbills in the pursuit of a clearly religious activity merely because the handbills invite the purchase of books for the improved understanding of the religion or because the handbills seek in a lawful fashion to promote the raising of funds for religious purposes."

In a five-to-four decision in 1942 the Court had upheld the constitutionality of a municipal ordinance imposing a license on book selling. But a year later in *Murdock v. Pennsylvania* the Court vacated its earlier decision in another five-to-four decision. This case clarified the right of a religious propagandist to call on householders who might or might not want to be bothered. The Court said:

> The fact that the ordinance is "nondiscriminatory" is immaterial. The protection afforded by the First Amendment is not so restricted. A license tax certainly does not acquire constitutional validity because it classifies the privileges protected by the First Amendment along with the wares and merchandise of hucksters and peddlers and treats them all alike. Such equality in treatment does not save the ordinance. Freedom of press, freedom of religion are in a preferred position.

Witness attorneys lost the *Chaplinsky v. New Hampshire* case in 1942. A Jehovah's Witness had been charged with creating a disturbance in Rochester, New Hampshire. He was carrying a placard proclaiming that religion is a racket. When apprehended the enraged Witness called the city marshal a "God-damned racketeer" and a "damned Fascist." He was convicted for violating a state statute against calling anyone "offensive" or "derisive" names in public. His conviction was upheld by the highest court, which decided that personal insults do not come under the constitutional protection of free speech.

In these and similar decisions the Supreme Court spelled out the rights of Jehovah's Witnesses and any other religious group to bring its message to the attention of the public. Other people were free to ignore the message, slam the door, tear up the handbills. The community, however, could not by law isolate its citizens from such undesired intrusions on their privacy or peace of mind. The Court cut the ground from under the so-called Green River ordinances which sought to forbid uninvited calls at private homes. The principle established by the Court was stated in *Martin v. City of Struthers* (1943):

> While door to door distributors of literature may be either a nuisance or a blind for criminal activities, they may also be useful members of society engaged in the dissemination of ideas in accordance with the best tradition of free discussion. The widespread use of this method of communication by many groups espousing various causes attests its major importance....
>
> Freedom to distribute information to every citizen wherever he desires to receive it is so clearly vital to the preservation of a free society that, putting aside reasonable police and health regulations of time and manner of distribution, it must be fully preserved.

A relatively recent innovation in Witness conduct spawned another series of court cases. Judge Rutherford had declared in 1935 that Jehovah's Witnesses could not in conscience salute the flag of the United States or any other worldly nation. To some extent this refusal was based on a literal interpretation of the commandment against bowing down before any graven image. In a deeper sense the Witnesses believed that such a salute would be an acknowledgment of loyalty and fealty to the government of the United States which they held to be nothing more than an instrument of Satan. For similar reasons Witnesses were and are counseled to remain seated during the playing of the national anthem. Until the nation edged closer toward involvement in war, the stand of the Witnesses was understood by the few who knew about it to be simply another cultic curiosity.

The matter was brought to the attention of a war-jittery nation when a school board in Minersville, Pennsylvania, expelled two Jehovah's Witnesses children for refusing to salute the American flag in a school assembly. Witness lawyers attacked the board's action as a violation of the due process clause of the Fourteenth Amendment. But in the celebrated *Minersville v. Gobitis* case the Supreme Court upheld the school board's action; only Justice Stone dissented.

This remained the law of the land for three years. Then in the *West Virginia State Board of Education v. Barnette* decision the Court reversed itself. Since then citizens have not been required by law to salute the flag of their nation. Three justices—Frankfurter, Roberts and Reed—disagreed and adhered to the earlier Gobitis decision. The majority opinion stated: "If there is any fixed star in our constitutional constellation, it is that no official, high or petty, can prescribe what shall be orthodox in politics, nationalism, religion, or other matters of opinion or force citizens to confess by word or act their faith therein."

Meanwhile public resentment against the cult, bolstered by the original 1940 Gobitis decision and fanned by growing fears of Nazi successes in Europe, prompted many citizens especially in small towns to take out their frustrations on Witness missionaries.

"Not since the persecution of the Mormons years ago has any religious minority been so bitterly and generally attacked as the members of Jehovah's Witnesses—particularly in the spring and summer of 1940," comments a pamphlet issued by the American Civil Liberties Union in January 1941.

During the single year 1940 the Witnesses and the ACLU filed documents with the Department of Justice describing 335 cases of mob violence in practically every state of the Union involving 1,488 men, women, and children. Covington has reported 2,500 mobbings of Witnesses between 1940 and 1944. Few incidents were reported from towns of more than 5,000 population, which supposedly enjoyed better police protection.

Ironically many agitators and hooligans charged the Witnesses with being Nazis or Fifth Columnists at the same time that thousands of German Witnesses were being herded into Hitler's concentration camps. They had refused to salute the swastika or render the Hitler salute.

In a statement signed by such prominent clergymen as Reinhold Niebuhr and Harry Emerson Fosdick, eight other Protestant ministers and a rabbi testified: "Nothing in the beliefs or practices of Jehovah's Witnesses justifies the charges of a lack of patriotism leveled against them." The clergymen meant well and wanted to forestall further mob action and violence. Nevertheless a better acquaintance with Witness theology might put the issue on some basis other than patriotism. If a Jehovah's Witness who refuses military service, shirks any public service, abstains from voting in any local or national election, sits during the national anthem, refuses to salute the flag, and damns his government as a tool of Satan can be considered "patriotic," who indeed is "unpatriotic"? The estrangement of the dedicated Witness obviously rules out "patriotism" as we know it and the only rights the Witnesses have ever claimed have been the basic rights of aliens living in a foreign country. They boast that they are patriotic only toward the Theocracy.

The ACLU writers who came to their defense also climbed out on a shaky limb with their assertion: "They have no creed but the Bible, no clergymen and no places of worship." If the Witnesses have no creed as such, their particular interpretation of the Bible certainly constitutes a religious system. Their basic plea for draft exemption rested on their claim that all baptized members were ordained ministers of the gospel and their thousands of Kingdom Halls were "places of worship" as much as any cathedral, synagogue, or chapel.

Typical of the many affidavits filed by Witnesses in the 1940 rash of disturbances is that of Albert Stroebel of Flagstaff, Arizona. He relates that he was accosted by three men while sitting on the porch of a friend. They demanded that he salute the flag. When he said he would not, they called him a "Nazi spy," beat him unconscious and dragged him across the street to a service station. An angry crowd gathered and began shouting "Heil Hitler," "String him up!" and "Chop his head off!" A deputy sheriff took him into protective custody and later drove him and his father to Prescott where they were released.

In Litchfield, Illinois, about 100 Witnesses came to town in a caravan of 21 automobiles to distribute literature and play their phonograph records. A mob destroyed 12 of the cars; 64 Witnesses were taken to a police station by the mob and beaten in attempts to force them to salute the flag.

An attack on a Kingdom Hall in Kennebunk, Maine, on September 9, 1940, climaxed several months of agitation. French Catholics resented the slurs on their religion by Witness preachers. Finally Witnesses retreated to their hall and fired on their assailants. One Witness was convicted of assault with intent to kill. Those arrested for burning the building were tried and acquitted.

In a nearby Maine Village, North Windham, a Witness tried to play his phonograph for a garage mechanic who did not wish to be bothered. The mechanic hit the Witness with a tire iron and in the scuffle that followed, the Witness pulled a gun and killed the mechanic.

Two female Witnesses, one seventy and the other in her fifties, in Connersville, Indiana, were found guilty of "riotous conspiracy" and sentenced to from two to ten years in the state prison. Their crime was actually refusing to salute the flag. The pair was convicted of a crime defined to cripple the once-powerful Ku Klux Klan in the state and aimed at "three or more persons who unite to do an unlawful act in the nighttime."

As the number of such incidents multiplied, Attorney General Francis Biddle made a nationwide appeal on a radio network:

"Members of a religious sect known as Jehovah's Witnesses have been repeatedly set upon and beaten. They had committed no crime; but the mob adjudged they had, and meted out mob punishment. The Attorney General has ordered an immediate investigation of these outrages.

"The people must be alert and watchful, and above all cool and sane. Since mob violence will make the government's task infinitely more difficult, it will not be tolerated. We shall not defeat the Nazi evil by emulating its methods."

To help pacify their tormentors the Witnesses devised a formula and pledge of respect for the flag which they said they would be willing to recite standing with their hats off.

I have pledged my unqualified allegiance and devotion to Jehovah the Almighty God and to his Kingdom for which Jesus commands all Christians to pray.

I respect the flag of the United States and acknowledge it as a symbol of freedom and justice for all. I pledge allegiance and obedience to all the laws of the United States that are consistent with God's laws as set forth in the Bible.

Jehovah's Witnesses deny they are pacifists since they would gladly take up arms in a holy war for Jehovah. Since their theology teaches that Witnesses themselves will only sit on a hillside and observe the carnage of the battle of Armageddon, this distinction seems rather academic. Unlike members of the historic peace churches such as the Mennonites and Brethren who will agree to serve as medical corpsmen or noncombatants, the Witnesses generally tried to claim exemption from the draft on the basis that they were ministers of the gospel. They claimed to see no distinction between a priest, monk, minister or rabbi and a Jehovah's Witness who worked 40 hours a week in a factory but visited homes at night and during spare hours. The draft boards did.

The Society took the position that any religious organization could decide who were qualified as ministers and who were not. No seminary course or formal ordination would be required if the denomination itself set up no such requirements.

The local draft boards and the courts naturally took a rather dim view of this line of argument. The courts eventually did exempt most of those full-time representatives who were certified by Brooklyn headquarters. Members of the Bethel family were also given exemptions on the same basis as Catholic monks.

General Hershey ruled that those working more than 80

hours a month in religious activities could claim 4D status. Nevertheless local boards often denied such classification to pioneers who were supposed to put in 150 hours a month. An issue of the *Cornell Studies in Civil Liberty* observed: "Rather consistently throughout the course of the war, Jehovah's Witnesses were more harshly treated in terms of sentences than other conscientious objectors, while conscientious objectors as a class received higher sentences than those violators of the Selective Service Act who did not claim to be conscientious objectors" (*Conscription of Conscience,* by Mulford Q. Sibley and Philip E. Jacob).

In the Falbo case the Supreme Court declared that a Jehovah's Witness must first comply with orders, be inducted and then come to a federal court for relief. Only Justice Murphy dissented. This decision by the highest court in 1944 destroyed the Society's basis for exemption for its members. Between 1941 and 1946, more than 4,300 Witnesses were imprisoned in federal penitentiaries. A number of Witnesses got the maximum sentences of five years and a $10,000 fine. Nearly three out of four prosecutions on draft evasion for religious reasons involved Witnesses.

Citizens who already disliked the Witnesses because of their abusive attacks on the churches and clergymen and their refusal to salute the flag now realized that members of the sect were seeking to escape the draft by what seemed to them to be the phony claim that they were all ordained ministers. The parents of a son fighting in North Africa or Saipan might be driven to unwise actions if they found out that a healthy neighbor boy, a Jehovah's Witness, was making good money in a defense plant and claiming ministerial status. Attacks on the sect continued. Attorney General Biddle again spoke out. In an address before the National Conference on Social Work in 1941 he said:

"We all know of the outrages committed against the members of the sect known as Jehovah's Witnesses, who, with the misplaced zeal of martyrs, openly tempt retaliation for their attacks on the Catholic Church, so that grand juries refuse to return indictments. Where state officials should have been active in preventing this cruel persecution, they have in many instances permitted it to occur, and in some cases have been the leaders of the mob. And this betrayal of the rights of citizens is done in the name of patriotism, and failure to salute the flag is made an excuse to desecrate the principles of which the flag is a symbol. The test of our ability to preserve these principles is always sharper in times of crisis. Hitler's methods cannot preserve our democracy, which demands justice for all alike."

While these thousands of Witnesses were incarcerated the federal government demanded that they submit to various vaccinations. Many Witnesses balked since they classed vaccinations with blood transfusions. They were one by one sent to solitary confinement until a representative of the Society from Brooklyn was allowed to talk to the Witness convicts for two hours to convince them that Jehovah had no objections to such inoculations. References in earlier Watchtower publications could easily have led members to assume that these were prohibited but this did not become an official policy.

After the war the Witnesses at their convention in Cleveland adopted a resolution asking the President to pardon some of the imprisoned Witnesses. The political weight of a group of people who do not vote is minimal. Finally 150 Witnesses did receive pardons out of a total of 1,523 pardons granted.

The test cases involving civil rights in religious proselytizing, flag saluting and draft exemptions no longer make the headlines but the sect's objection to blood transfusions continues to provide news stories every year. The prohibition against blood transfusions was made official in the *Watchtower* of July 1, 1945. The Witness moralists quoted various passages in Genesis and Leviticus against the eating of blood, which they interpreted to mean blood transfusions (Genesis 9:4; Leviticus 3:17, 7:27, and 17:10, 11, and 14). Neither the 11,000,000 Jews or 800,000,000 Christians understood these passages to prohibit what was obviously unknown to the people of the Old Testament. Nor did the Witnesses or Russellites object to the treatment before 1945. Now agreeing to such a transfusion is considered a serious sin against Jehovah and an action deserving disfellowshiping by the congregation.

In 1951 a Jehovah's Witness mother refused to authorize a transfusion for her child who was suffering from a ruptured appendix. Another mother in Chicago objected to a recommended transfusion for her daughter because, she said, "We can't break Jehovah's law." In both cases the courts decided to take the child away from its natural parents, administer the transfusion, and return the child.

The father and two brothers of the victim of an automobile accident in Texas in 1952 stood guard in her hospital room to prevent doctors from giving a transfusion. Her physician predicted death if she did not get it. Finally doctors called the police, who arrested the three men on the grounds of disturbing the peace. The woman's divorced husband got a court injunction restraining the family from interfering with the transfusion. The woman herself was not a Witness.

Again in 1952 a Witness mother gave birth to a baby with an incompatible Rh factor. Doctors agreed that without an immediate transfusion the baby would either die or suffer irreparable mental damage. The court appointed a guardian who consented to the transfusion.

The Watchtower Society indoctrinates its adherents in the view that they live as aliens in all worldly societies. They owe no special allegiance to the country in which they labor as representatives of the Theocracy. But as "aliens" they show no hesitation in appealing to the police and courts of the nation, a nation which unlike the New World Society is nothing but the political tool of Jehovah's adversary: Satan. The Society made it a matter of policy to appeal every adverse decision even up to the Supreme Court. Twice the Supreme Court itself has reversed its own earlier decisions in cases involving Jehovah's Witnesses.

Much of their remarkable legal success can be attributed to the fact that for 25 years the tiny sect was headed by a small-town lawyer-turned-prophet who in turn groomed a brilliant Texan to become one of the top constitutional experts in the nation. Hayden Covington was born in Texas in 1911 and graduated from the San Antonio School of Law in 1933. He took up Witness preaching the next year and joined the Brooklyn legal staff in 1939, becoming a member of the New York bar.

Recently Covington resigned from the Society's board of directors, saying that he was only one of the "other sheep." All the other members of the Watchtower boards claim to be members of the remnant who expect to rule with Jesus Christ in heaven as spirit creatures.

During most of the Witness litigation the only Roman

Catholic on the Supreme Court, Justice Frank Murphy, could usually be found upholding the liberal interpretation of the First and Fourteenth Amendments to the advantage of the Witnesses. Murphy, a member of a church which the Watchtower constantly branded as the "whore of Babylon" and the "clerical-fascist mob," would declare in 1944:

> . . . From ancient times to the present day, the ingenuity of man has known no limits in its ability to forge weapons of oppression for use against those who dare to express or practice unorthodox religious beliefs. And the Jehovah's Witnesses are living proof of the fact that even in this nation, conceived as it was in the ideals of freedom, the right to practice religion in unconventional ways is still far from secure. Theirs is a militant and unpopular faith, pursued with fanatical zeal. They have suffered brutal beatings; their property has been destroyed; they have been harassed at every turn by the resurrection and enforcement of little used ordinances and statutes. . . . To them, along with other present-day religious minorities, befalls the burden of testing our devotion to the ideals and constitutional guarantees of religious freedom.

If Roman Catholic Murphy received no gratitude for his forthright stand for religious freedom, neither did the American Civil Liberties Union, the Society's legal ally in many a battle. The ACLU remained simply an instrument of Satan which for reasons no Witness could fathom chose to help the New World Society against the principalities and powers of the state.

President Knorr says the Witnesses are "glad for all to make use of these freedom-assuring victories, because they favor freedom for all, not just themselves. To disagree is not intolerant; to gag those who do disagree with you is intolerant." [3]

The sect's considerable success in the courts should convince orthodox Christians that the value of martyrdom whether in Rome's Colosseum or Jersey City's street corners cannot be overestimated. The Witnesses wore the cloak of the underdog with a measure of eagerness. In many cases the most sympathetic observer would have to admit that the Witnesses asked for it. It took more than general appeals to tolerance to pacify a Catholic crowd which watched out-of-town Witnesses parading in front of their parish church with RELIGION IS A RACKET signs on Sunday morning.

A fistfight or arrest put the Witnesses in the category of the persecuted while the provocation was forgotten. Drawing its new blood from those elements in society which made up the dispossessed and the proletariat, the Society could bring itself to their attention by such incidents. Here were simple people being oppressed by the same clerical and political powers which oppress me, thought the bystander with proletarian tendencies.

The by-product of all these riots, outrages, arrests, forced flag salutings, and court cases was a spelling out of constitutional freedoms for all Americans. What all Americans can applaud is the affirmation by the highest court that religious bodies may present their message to the public regardless of the popularity or unpopularity of the group and its doctrines. For this we can thank the Witnesses of Jehovah and their canny and persistent lawyers.

12. *Who Joins the New World Society?*

To WHAT PEOPLE does the Watchtower make its strongest appeal? What sort of person listens to the message of Armageddon with sympathy and decides to enlist under the banner of the Theocracy? How does his decision affect his life and that of his family?

Reliable statistical information which would throw light on these questions is scarce. Brooklyn discourages surveys of the membership by outsiders. Students of the movement must rely on observation, personal interviews with willing Witnesses, and official publications of the Society to reach at least partial answers.

Probably the best analysis of the sect's membership patterns and appeals to date has been made by Werner Cohn, who studied the Watchtower as a graduate student at the New School for Social Research. His master's thesis formed the basis for an article in *The American Scholar* entitled "Jehovah's Witnesses as a Proletarian Sect" (Summer, 1955).

Cohn characterizes the New World Society as a proletarian sect in the original, non-Communist meaning of the term "proletarian." This definition means an individual or group which is spiritually disattached from the larger social organism. He feels out of place in his society, outside its power structure. On a political level he dismisses the society as bourgeois; on a religious level he might conclude that the society which has excluded him from its privileges and advantages is simply the visible kingdom of Satan.

Cohn observes:

> The Witnesses are actually separated by an almost airtight spiritual barrier from the rest of American society—the organization is a universe unto itself.

If we accept Cohn's analysis of the basic proletarian orientation of the Watchtower we will look for success by Witness proselytizers among those groups in society which consider themselves outside of the mainstream of that society. An earlier critic, Ferguson, put it this way:

> Here in modern times is a religion which expresses, flagrantly and belligerently, a dreadful sense of mass inferiority.[1]

Through temperament, race, or economic disadvantage certain subgroups stand apart from the power struggles, cultural interests, political debates and economic battles of other people. Those groups which come closest to the American equivalent of the proletariat—the Negro, the poor and unemployable, the Puerto Rican and Spanish-American—have provided many of the recent converts to the New World Society. Other recruits have been drawn from marginal Roman Catholics with traditional anticlerical tendencies, such as some Italians, French, and Spanish. Some Witnesses come out of the fundamentalist sects which have started to flirt with more liberal biblical interpretations.

As mankind continues to live under the sword of the H-bomb and as mankind's problems multiply in number and complexity, many simple folk give up all hope of understanding the ways of the world. They survey the world scene and throw up their hands in despair and disgust. To them the pages of the *Watchtower* and *Awake!* whisper, "Leave Satan's old wicked world. These troubles have all been foretold thousands of years ago in the Bible. We have the key to understand these prophecies. The end is near for the present masters: the proud clergymen, the grafting politicians, the selfish capitalists." The zealous Witness publisher urges, "Join a clean New World Society ruled by Jehovah God through his 'woman,' the Watchtower Society. Flee to the ark of safety and escape destruction at Armageddon."

Typically the prospective convert will first meet a Witness missionary at his doorstep. He need not leave his living room. Whereas most Protestant ministers would expect him to attend a revival or church service where sanctimonious ushers pass the plate and eye his clothing, this friendly minister simply asks for the opportunity to spend a few minutes explaining some Bible texts. He offers to return and devote as many hours as necessary to outline the beliefs of this New World Society which claims to base all its teachings on God's holy word.

Even though the Watchtower minister may work all day in a factory or on a farm, he displays an ability to marshal dozens of Bible passages to support his doctrines. He outlines the magnitude of the Watchtower Society's world-wide operations, mentions the size of the magazine circulations, uses the growth of the Society during the past two decades to bolster his claims to Jehovah's exclusive favor.

Eventually the Witness minister reveals that not only can the convert join the clean New World Society and escape Armageddon's fury, but he can qualify as an ordained minister himself! Think of that! No need to attend a theological seminary or even produce a high school diploma. By diligent study of the Bible and Watchtower publications and attendance at meetings at the local Kingdom Hall he can qualify for baptism and ministerial standing. He need not give up his job. In a few months he himself can go forth to call on his neighbors and expound the wonders of the Theocracy and the intricate prophecies of the Bible in their living rooms. The appeal of this promised status in a booming, world-wide Society should not be underestimated.

Should the prospect be a Negro, he can be invited to an interracial congregation or circuit assembly to see a practical demonstration of the no-segregation policy now enforced, at least in northern states. A Puerto Rican or Mexican-American, nominally Roman Catholic, finds he can understand the Spanish-speaking Witness and read the Bible and Watchtower magazines in his own language. The Latin Mass was more or less familiar but still mysterious and the local pastor and parishioners may not have spoken Spanish or gone out of their way to welcome a dark-skinned newcomer to their parish. The Italian-American may have stopped attending Mass years ago but has never become a Protestant because no one showed much interest in his religious views.

Ferguson comments:

Here are farmers, barbers, grocers, eking out an unwelcome life in sordid circumstances. Through correct belief in the words of Holy Writ, as interpreted by their leader, they have become the sons and daughters of God awaiting the return of the conquering angel and the establishment of themselves in high places.[2]

As the convert enters the life of the New World Society he cuts the ties which once bound him and his family to the larger community. In Watchtower books he reads, "Association in a social way with those outside the truth is dangerous." [3] His former friends, co-workers and relatives shake their heads at his new religious zeal. He spends several nights a week in Kingdom Hall, most of his spare hours in his preaching work. Perhaps his Catholic kinfolk begin novenas and light candles for his soul. Soon he discovers that most of his friends are those he meets at Kingdom Hall who, like him, are "in the truth."

If he has been active in a labor union, lodge, veterans' organization, civic group or political organization he either drops his membership or retains only passive interest. He may keep his union card as a form of "job insurance" but the Society advises: "A Christian should not get involved in union activity to the extent of holding an official position in the union. Nor, in the event of a strike, should he take part in picketing or in other ways agitate for the cause of the strike." He should become a neutral in politics and a neutral in the "governing activities and economic warfare of the union." [4]

He no longer observes such "pagan" celebrations as Christmas, Easter, Halloween or the birthday anniversaries of members of his family. The Society quotes Jeremiah to damn Christmas trees as a heathenish custom: "The customs of the people are vanity; for one cutteth a tree out of the forest, the work of the hands of the workman with an axe. They deck it with silver and gold."

The Society does not prohibit moderate smoking and drinking but the informed Witness knows that these habits only enslave men and waste money. No one living at Bethel may smoke. The *Watchtower* warns: "You must be clean from the stain and stench of the tobacco weed." [5] An issue of *Awake!* explains, "The use of tobacco decreases such mental faculties as memory, concentration and will power, as well as our physical powers of endurance." [6] It assures its readers that there will be no cigarettes or cigars in the New World after Armageddon.

Witnesses oppose total abstinence as a test of Christian faith and reject prohibition as an answer to the liquor problem. Unlike the Methodists and many Holiness sects, the Witnesses serve ordinary red wine at their annual communion service. "What the Bible condemns is the misuse of wine. Nowhere in the Scriptures is there a condemnation of wine itself." [7]

The Witness avoids movies, dances, card playing, radio and TV, boxing and wrestling matches (such amusements appeal to the depraved and killer instincts in man, according to the December 8, 1960, issue of *Awake!*). "In your secular employment, as far as possible avoid all compromising situations, such as Christmas parties, business conventions and union outings, which are so notorious for their moral laxity. Have no part in the gambling and drinking matches of employees or business associates. You must be clean from immorality and loose conduct. You must be clean from drunkenness and excesses. You must be clean in speech and mouth, free from vulgar oaths and obscene profanity." [8] These entertainments and habits distract the Witness from his main and urgent job of advertising the Kingdom and warning his neighbors about the end of things.

The convert takes a reasonable interest in his health and encounters no health taboos except those against hypnotism, sterilization, blood transfusions and psychiatry. An *Awake!* article in the February 22, 1961, issue entitled "Hypnosis: A Dangerous Two-Edged Sword" called the practice sinister, ill-advised, dangerous and unscriptural. Several articles and news items a year appear in *Watchtower* publications about blood transfusions. No one would argue with the statement in the January 15, 1961, *Watchtower*: "Blood transfusions were not in vogue in apostolic days" (p. 63). Not many non-Witnesses would be able to agree with the rest of the article, including statements such as: "God's law definitely says that the soul of man is in his blood. Hence the receiver of the blood transfusion is feeding upon a God-given soul as contained in the blood vehicle of a fellow man or of fellow men" (p. 64). The Witness who agrees to a tranfusion risks being disfellowshiped by the congregation.

In answer to a question about the legitimacy of sterilization the December 1, 1961, issue of the *Watchtower* made it clear that it views all sterilization—eugenic, therapeutic, and punitive—as contrary to the will of Jehovah. If a woman's health or a family's budget would be ruined by another child, the *Watchtower* recommended not contraception but self-control. "When a Christian understands the good purpose for which self-control must be exercised then it appears to him reasonable and he is strengthened to exercise it, with the aid of God's spirit." [8]

This stand would seem to indicate a hardening attitude of Jehovah's Witnesses against birth control. In *A Guide to the Religions of America* Milton G. Henschel, Knorr's executive aid, said: "Jehovah's Witnesses regard birth control as an entirely personal matter." [9] Now the Society has declared that even such serious reasons as health and poverty do not justify recourse to sterilization or contraception.

During the summer and fall of 1961 the Watchtower Society extended the prohibition against blood transfusion to a general prohibition against the eating of blood in meats. Since the transfusion ban was based on an interpretation of Old Testament injunctions against the eating of blood, it was probably inevitable that the Witnesses would get around to stricter dietary laws regarding blood. Before this pronouncement the average Witness household ate whatever it desired.

Now the Society quoted a passage, "Flesh with its soul—its blood—you must not eat (Genesis 9:4)," to warn the faithful against eating meat improperly slaughtered or prepared. "Meat can be eaten, but not with the blood still in it, because the blood represents the soul or life of the creature. Man must show respect for the sanctity of blood, and, so doing, show his respect for the Lifegiver, Jehovah God." So reported the *Watchtower* for September 15, 1961 (p. 554).

Witnesses were instructed to ask their butcher whether the animals and fowl he sold had been properly drained of their blood when killed. Anything strangled or improperly drained has to be avoided. Likewise Witnesses were told not to patronize restaurants which do not serve meat which has been prepared according to the ancient laws.

The faithful were especially warned against such items as blood sausage, rare beef, hamburger, weiners and cold cuts which often contain mixtures of meat, fat and blood. Devout Witnesses will probably begin to patronize kosher markets and restaurants to avoid risking the eating of blood.

Even drugs manufactured with animal or human blood must be rejected.

The September 15, 1960, issue of the *Watchtower* reaffirmed the stand against transfusions. It quoted a Dr. Alonzo Jay Shadman who warned, "The poisons that produce the impulse to commit suicide, murder, or steal are in the blood." The same article quotes a Brazilian physician who maintains that "moral insanity, sexual perversion, repression, inferiority complexes and petty crimes" often follow in the wake of blood transfusions (p. 564).

An *Awake!* writer concludes that 99 times out of 100 the mentally disturbed Jehovah's Witness should consult a mature Witness rather than a worldly psychiatrist.

> Often when a Witness of Jehovah goes to a psychiatrist, the psychiatrist will try to persuade him that his troubles are caused by his religion, entirely overlooking the fact that the Christian witnesses of Jehovah are the best-oriented, happiest, and most contented group of people on the face of the earth.[10]

Only adultery may be presented as a legitimate cause for divorce; any other reason for divorce subjects the husband and wife to expulsion from the congregation. Any Witness known to have committed fornication or adultery may be put on probation or expelled.

The Witness parent will obey the law and send his children to grade and high school but he will probably try to discourage any ideas they may have about college. College years are years which could be better spent in preaching the Kingdom. In four years Armageddon may have ushered in the New World. Souls which might have been saved were annihilated because uppity children thought they needed to study English and psychology and philosophy in some college.

The Witness seldom bothers with the PTA or school board elections or school bond issues since he does not vote and does not wish to get entangled in worldly affairs. His children may endure some embarrassment in school for refusing to salute the flag, stand for the national anthem or participate in Christmas festivities but the legal justification for these positions has been established by the highest court.

The devout Witness family begins the day by reading the daily scripture text in the current *Yearbook.* Close reading of the *Watchtower* and *Awake!* and new books as they are issued enables the family to join in the catechism question-and-answer sessions in Kingdom Hall. The family continues its study of the Bible with the official New World translations which confirm special Witness interpretations more than Protestant and Catholic versions.

The Society makes few if any demands on the family pocketbook for charitable causes. It supports no charities. Once in a while the brethren may be asked to donate used clothing or money to help distressed Witnesses such as the victims of the Chilean earthquake. The Witness would not be inclined to contribute to a Community Chest or United Fund campaign.

The Watchtower no longer counsels against marriage but Cohn observes: "Wherever Witness literature and organizational structure touch upon the theme of sex, an attempt is made to banish sexual activity completely from the lives of Witnesses." [11] Judge Rutherford used to ask his followers to postpone marriage since the precious days before Armageddon were too few to squander on private pleasures. Echoes of this advice can be heard in current literature:

Standing now at the threshold of Jehovah's new world, many

youths may want to postpone marriage until after Armageddon, when selection of a wife will be made under righteous conditions and when marriage responsibilities will be carried out with none of the distractions that now plague mankind. . . . With the rapid approach of Armageddon, youths of the New World society should want to seize hold of the grand privilege that is theirs, that is, to give their all for the sake of the Kingdom, thus safeguarding their position at this time of the end.[12]

Most Witnesses, however, follow the example of Russell, Rutherford and Knorr and get married.

Some students of the sect such as Professor Herbert Stroup of Brooklyn College believe that the rate of domestic breakups is higher among Witnesses than among non-Witnesses. The adjustment in family living in a situation in which one mate joins the Witnesses and the other remains a practicing Catholic, Protestant or Jew creates obvious tensions.

The Watchtower tries to head off mixed marriages:

There are many dedicated Christian girls who would like to marry this side of Armageddon, but there appears to be a scarcity of good, clean eligible mates. What should these do? Should they reach out beyond the congregation of God to get themselves a companion not dedicated to the doing of Jehovah's will? Some have done so to their sorrow. The Scriptural injunction is: Marry "only in the Lord." (I Cor. 7:39) True, the single state may impose a great test of faith on many, but enduring trials for righteousness' sake brings God's blessing. One who seeks the company of outsiders may end up marrying out of the truth. Trials arising out of such mixed marriages come as a result of ignoring God's counsel.[13]

Most religious faiths advise against interreligious marriages but the Watchtower Society must ask some of its women members to remain celibate rather than seek a mate "outside of the truth." There are just not enough unmarried male Witnesses to go around. (When the Mormons found themselves in this predicament they encouraged polygamy, but this could hardly be recommended by the Watchtower today.)

Like other proletarian sects, the Watchtower promotes the use of a special language which serves as a form of social cohesion. The Witness knows what a fellow Witness means when he speaks of someone "in the truth." He knows what is meant by "God's woman," "the remnant," "the anointed," the "bride of Christ," etc. To the outsider these terms may mean little or may be taken to mean orthodox Christian concepts, but to the initiated they signify an esoteric knowledge of Jehovah's own mysteries. Even the intonation can mark a Witness, just as the long *a* pronunciation of Mary Baker Eddy usually identifies a member of the Christian Science church.

Once committed to the New World Society, the Witness values his standing in the congregation above every other relationship and avoids whatever might threaten this relationship. Should he backslide or violate the mores of the Society he may be disfellowshiped, in which case his fellow Witnesses would allow him to continue to attend Kingdom Hall meetings but would neither speak to him nor associate with him. He might incur such excommunication by divorcing his mate for any reason but adultery, failing to meet his preaching obligations, mixing too much with outsiders, drinking excessively, committing fornication, stirring up discontent, or harboring heretical ideas. During 1958–59 the Society reported that 6,552 people were disfellowshiped, many for fornication and adultery. But 1,597 of these or other disfellowshiped members were reinstated on proof of repentance.[14]

Estimates of the percentage of Witnesses in the United States who are Negroes range from 20 per cent to 30 per cent. At any rate, the proportion is considerably higher than among the general population. To date no Negro has broken into the upper echelons of the Brooklyn hierarchy although many Negroes have graduated from Gilead. Proselytizing among a group of Americans already estranged to some degree from the mainstream of community life has brought impressive results.

During Judge Rutherford's years, Negroes attended their own segregated international assemblies. Many cities, especially in the South, still maintain separate white and Negro Kingdom Halls. Lest Witnesses take advantage of the relative social freedom in northern congregations, *Awake!* has recently counseled against interracial marriages.[15]

If the Society now enforces racial equality, it has never thought much of women's rights and places women Witnesses in a subservient position in the congregation and the larger Society. They may not hold any congregational office, much less an office in the Watchtower Society itself. They are warned not to try to contradict or correct the brothers in Kingdom Hall meetings. They may not teach or preach from the platform to the congregation. They are told that the husband is the head of the house. Since he is the head, the Society has stated that he may dictate the religion of his children. If his wife is a dedicated Witness she must nevertheless allow her husband to raise the children as Catholics or Methodists or Jews if that is his wish.[16] Women are held to be weaker than men and a continual source of temptation and distraction. They can always bring up Mrs. Russell as a case in point.

Limited observation indicates that the Witnesses still attract a disproportionate percentage of converts from the lower and lower-middle classes. Father McCluskey lists some of the candidates for the New World:

> . . . the bitter from whom life has stolen hope, the malcontent or anarchical who are eaten up with disgust at government, the business failures who have been bruised in competition. There are the simplest lovers of *the* Book who yearn for more knowledge of it and who are assured that Jehovah's mighty truth lies plainly before their eyes, if only they will keep staring at what they are told is there.
>
> In the market place there will always be crowds of the simple, the illiterate, the dejected, the novelty seekers, the underprivileged, and the genuinely hungry for God to buy the wares of the Father Divines, Brother Robertses, Prophet Joneses, Sister Aimees and the Jehovah's Witnesses.

But the caliber of membership in the Society seems to be rising. Some recruits have been baptized from the ranks of white-collar workers, craftsmen, physicians, although most Witnesses continue to engage in factory work, farming and unskilled labor. Hardly any hold college degrees; one midwestern state university with more than 16,000 students lists only one Jehovah's Witness in its student body. The sect has been called a religion of the "economically and socially disinherited."

Interviews with Witnesses attending the mammoth 1958 assembly in New York City reveal diverse backgrounds. For example, there was Dr. F. D. Roylance, secretary of the medical executive committee of an Englewood, New Jersey, hospital. A former Disciple of Christ and Congregationalist, the doctor received Watchtower tracts from one of his patients, studied them and asked for baptism in 1956. He admitted, "My wife is very much opposed to all this. She is

Italian, but her father took the family out of the Roman Catholic Church before they came to this country. She still goes to the Congregational Church, and she resents very much the time that this takes from my work and our three children." He said he would prescribe a blood transfusion for a non-Witness.

Mr. and Mrs. Wildred Childs, both in their late twenties, came to the assembly from their home in York Harbor, Maine. He works as an automobile mechanic, has trouble with his sight and hearing. His wife earns $40 a week taking care of an invalid woman. Mrs. Childs had been raised in French Canada as a Catholic but "never went to church much." A Witness publisher called at her home and introduced her to the sect's teachings. Her husband, who had been a Methodist, joined the Society later. Together they travel 12 miles to Portsmouth, New Hampshire, three times a week for Kingdom Hall meetings, study the Bible together, make door-to-door calls.

From Alaska came Otto Smith, thirty-three, who was raised a Baptist in Texas but left the Church during the war. "I was a gunner on B-24s stationed in England and flying over Germany," he said. "Before every mission the Protestant, Catholic and Jewish chaplains would get us together and pray. And I kept thinking how over there on the other side the ministers and priests were doing the same things. 'How can God listen to all of them' I kept asking myself. It wasn't until I came in contact with the Witnesses that I understood He wasn't listening to any of them." A Jehovah's Witness called at his door while he was selling automobiles in Anchorage. He and his wife were baptized in 1952.

Marcus Bach of the State University of Iowa has called the Witnesses "hypnotized people." Almost all adult Witnesses fall into the category of fairly recent converts. They display an infectious enthusiasm which cradle members of any religion find hard to duplicate. They have found a security and fellowship in the New World Society which they believed the old secular, indifferent world and the traditional churches never offered. The Society makes no great demands on their intellect after they give one total "yes" from their will.

They enjoy prestige within their own group, notice their self-improvement as speakers and Bible students, discover new abilities in argumentation. Like the skid-row bum, the Trappist monk, the hermit, they no longer worry about the world and its problems. They have resigned from society to join the cleaner, better New World Society. They expect to maintain their citizenship in this Society forever.

13. *Schisms and Heresies*

FEW RELIGIOUS MOVEMENTS spring into life without the help of theological midwives. Fewer still manage to escape subsequent schisms and heresies.

Denominations find a schism on their hands when one or more members refuse to go along with what they consider backsliding or error and manage to win others to their view. Sometimes this protest expresses the anguish of the conservatives who become convinced that essential doctrines are being slighted or denied. Occasionally the protestors desert the mother church as hopelessly reactionary and stagnant.

For example, Mormonism embraces not only the main Utah church but the Reorganized branch with headquarters in Independence, Missouri. The Missouri Mormons balked at following Brigham Young and embracing such doctrines as plural marriage. The Wesleyan revival reintroduced the spirit of Franciscanism into the coldly Calvinistic Church of England but Methodism itself would spawn dozens of other sects such as the Church of the Nazarene, the Free and Wesleyan Methodist churches, the Salvation Army, etc. In turn, the Salvation Army gave rise to the Volunteers of America; and so the wheel turns.

Jehovah's Witnesses are no exception. Thousands of Pastor Russell's converts could not swallow Judge Rutherford's innovations in doctrine and discipline. From time to time congregations would split into opposing factions or whole congregations would abandon the main corporate body to pursue what they deemed primitive Russellism.

Largest of these dissidents is the Dawn Bible Students Association of East Rutherford, New Jersey. Sponsors of the "Frank and Ernest" radio program on more than 300 stations every week, the Association claims to maintain the Pastor's original doctrines in their entirety and purity. The Dawn Bible Students even cling to the generally discredited Great Pyramid Theory; one of the Judge's reforms was to throw out this type of speculation.

Their monthly 64-page magazine *The Dawn* goes to 19,000 subscribers, a drop in the bucket in Watchtower terms but a substantial circulation for a tiny sect which is not even listed in the authoritative *Yearbook of American Churches.* Editions of the magazine are also published in French, Greek, Danish, German, Italian and Ukranian.

The Dawnites produce 15- and 30-minute TV programs carried by 16 U. S. stations. They continue to distribute Pastor Russell's original *Studies in the Scriptures* (1916 edition). They sell volumes one to six at 50 or 85 cents a copy in hard back but refuse to touch the controversial seventh volume issued posthumously by the Rutherford regime. Jehovah's Witnesses long ago gave up reprinting the Pastor's voluminous scriptural commentaries although Rutherford once applauded them as superior to all previous commentaries. The Dawnites also publish a series of pamphlets in all the languages in which the magazine is translated as well as Lithuanian, Polish, Roumanian, Hungarian, Hebrew, Slovak, Finnish, Spanish and Swedish.

Essentially the Dawnites represent Russellism as it was taught prior to the Pastor's death in 1916. Like the Witnesses they are Arians, denying the divinity of Christ. They too deny the existence of hell. But unlike the Witnesses, they discourage animosity toward other Christian churches and clergymen. They offer their teachings to all who will listen but should they bump into opposition they smile and move on, confident that these doubters will get a second chance to embrace the truth in the resurrection of the dead.

As Judge Rutherford consolidated his position in the Watchtower Society a number of "old timers" rebelled against the increasing tempo of the preaching campaigns, the quota system of book selling, the growing attention paid to organizational work and statistics and record keeping. Kindly souls objected to the increasingly vicious attacks on other Christians, particularly Roman Catholics and clergymen.

Dogmatic technicalities disturbed some veteran Russellites. Pastor Russell had taught that Jesus died for all men, but in 1939 the Judge announced that Adam himself was not redeemed and hence will not be raised from the dead. To most Witnesses this new interpretation made little difference. But recent converts could adapt their thinking on these points with less difficulty than those who remembered the Pastor and continued to consult his writings.

Today the Dawnites write:

These friends [Jehovah's Witnesses] are still earnest, sincere, and zealous. Would that all of us had the same degree of zeal; but the pure truth is no longer with them. They have some details of truth. They can define the soul; they believe in one God instead of three; they have a general knowledge that we are in the end of the age; but their central theme is not of God. They are laying down their lives bearing witness to a message which, according to their own viewpoint, is doing nothing for the masses who do not receive it except to make them liable to the second death. Thus has the sacred flame of truth—that inspiring truth of God's love revealed by ransom and restitution—been extinguished in the minds of many.[1]

During the late 1920's enough of the brethren had deserted the Watchtower to form a separate congregation in Pittsburgh, cradle of the movement. In October 1929 this congregation and a few other disaffected Bible Students came together in a convention. Another ecclesia in Brooklyn joined the schism. The infant organization launched an ambitious broadcasting effort which was soon to be curtailed during the depression. Meanwhile listeners had been invited to send in for free literature, and many responded. This literature had to be written and published. The first issue of *The Dawn* appeared.

As the movement slowly spread and others left the security of the Watchtower the elders were encouraged to renew radio evangelism. They began a new series of programs in 1940. This time the funds were available and the sect began to transcribe programs for rebroadcast in this country, Canada, Australia, and England.

Each year the members of the Dawn Bible Students Association elect 12 trustees who in turn choose the officers of the Association. To avoid empire building, no officer may hold the same office for more than two years. No dues or contributions are required for membership. Local ecclesias remain autonomous. The East Rutherford central office only supplies the literature, radio and TV programs and traveling lecturers to enable the local congregations to carry on their work and spread the gospel of Russellism. Observers cannot help but notice that the Dawnites display more intellectual interests, tolerance and sociability than their Witness cousins.

Some of the Dawnites' theological disagreements with the Witnesses may be summarized as follows. Dawnites teach that all men, good and wicked, will be given a second chance to accept the truth after death, whereas the Witnesses deny that any of the incorrigibly wicked will be resurrected. Dawnites deny the Watchtower teaching that the new world after Armageddon will be repopulated by the children of Jehovah's Witnesses who survive the battle. Dawnites hold the father of the race, Adam, in higher regard than the Witnesses and believe he has a chance at salvation. Dawnites deny the authority of the Theocracy functioning through the Watchtower Bible and Tract Society. Dawnites attach less importance to the need to sell books, call on householders, obtain magazine subscriptions, in order to be saved. Dawnites respect the free choice of the nonbeliever to reject their message while the Witnesses brand such refusal as fitting the refusers for annihilation. The Dawnites see nothing wrong with blood transfusions:

> . . . We see that there is no similarity at all between the ancient custom of drinking blood, which was forbidden by the Lord, and the modern science of blood transfusion. Therefore, only by definitely misapplying the Scriptures can they be construed to forbid deriving benefit from this very humane application of medical science. No one should permit such a flagrant misapplication of God's commands to deter him from receiving the benefits of blood transfusion through fear of disobeying God and of being sentenced to the "second death." [2]

A far more radical schism erupted in 1943 when a group of Jehovah's Witnesses established the Servants of Yah. They decided that Jehovah was actually the name of the devil. The name of God is Yah. Clearly then the Witnesses were servants of Satan.

The mysterious Servants of Yah claim to have arrived at a special esoteric knowledge of the Bible by reading the original Hebrew text and ignoring the commonly used vowel points. The initiates then substitute other vowel points known only to themselves. According to the Servants of Yah only 144,000 people were ever destined to discover the hidden meaning of the Scriptures. They cloak their activities in secrecy and receive mail at a G.P.O. number in Brooklyn.

The Servants of Yah see the Bible as nothing but prophecy, all of which relates to the present day. They explain: "The original text consisted of consonants only, but became buried beneath the Jewish vowel points, which made the text read quite differently. By the use of these vowel points the ancient Jews were able to manufacture and weave into the text their many 'fables and genealogies,' while the true message was lost. In the New Testament, the living Yah has hidden His message in a Hebrew text within the Greek." The Servants deny Armageddon, the Genesis flood, the existence of Satan, and the value of water baptism.

At least a dozen tiny groups using the general name of Associated Bible Students propagate Pastor Russell's views and usually claim exclusive authority to interpret these doctrines. The oldest of these traces its history to the changeover from Russell to Rutherford. Those who opposed Rutherford grouped themselves under the name Associated Bible Students or sometimes Berean Bible Students. They worked through the Pastoral Bible Institute chartered in 1918.

Until 1960 the Institute maintained its headquarters in the Watchtower's own bailiwick, Brooklyn. Today the Pastoral Bible Institute is located in St. Louis, Missouri (P.O. Box 3252, Couteau Station). Congregations of Associated Bible Students are autonomous but maintain fellowship with other congregations. Fraternal relations are maintained also with similar groups in England and Australia. They call their ministers elders.

The Pastoral Bible Institute publishes a monthly 16-page magazine, *The Herald of Christ's Kingdom,* which carries notices of regional conventions and itineraries of speakers connected with the Institute. Like Jehovah's Witnesses, the Associated Bible Students meet for the annual Memorial Supper on the 14th of Nisan.

The May 1961 edition lists 19 speakers, including the seven directors of the Pastoral Bible Institute. The Institute does not attempt to control the presentations of each of these speakers after the manner of the Watchtower Society. In fact, it explains:

> The brethren whose appointments are listed below are believed to be loyal to the Word of God, clear in its fundamental teachings, and in general harmony with the spirit and purpose of the Institute's ministry. However, this should not be understood as implying that they, any more than our Editorial Committee, endorse each and every expression appearing in this journal. Nor does it mean that our Institute endorses each and every expression to which they may give utterance in their discourses. Those to whom they minister are counseled to prove all things and to hold fast that which is good.

Delegates from many of these Russellite sects meet annually in a Unity Convention of Bible Students. They attempt to distribute their own tracts at the mammoth conventions of Jehovah's Witnesses and try to persuade Witnesses to go back to pure Russellism. The growth of the Watchtower Society would suggest that few Witnesses bother to investigate the claims of the more orthodox Russellites. To most modern Witnesses Pastor Russell is simply a name in the official history of the Society; they have probably never read a single book or tract by the founder of the movement.

More annoying to the Watchtower are the activities of an ex-Witness, William J. Schnell, who has written two books "exposing" the Society and its doctrines. He now lectures widely in Protestant churches and publishes a bimonthly magazine entitled *The Converted Jehovah's Witness Expositor* in Youngstown, Ohio.

Schnell joined the Society in Germany where he had been taken by his parents. They were stranded there by the outbreak of World War I. He left Lutheranism to become a Bible Student and worked at German headquarters at the Magdeburg Bethel. Schnell returned to the United States in 1927 and drifted away from the Society for a number of years. Back in the fold, he became a full-time pioneer, unit servant in Manhattan, and finally zone servant in Ohio and Pennsylvania. He organized 85 new congregations and baptized 463 converts but left the Watchtower Society for good in 1954. His main apologetic effort is now concentrated in evangelical Protestant groups and he tries to instruct Protestants in ways to refute Witness missionaries and win them to orthodox Christianity. He claims to have brought more than 7,100 Jehovah's Witnesses back to the traditional churches. His first book, *Thirty Years a Watch Tower Slave,* has gone into seven printings.

Just as we have seen how the Watchtower Society has given

birth to a cluster of minor sects, we might spend a minute to examine the denomination from which it borrowed its chief doctrinal emphasis: adventism. Russell relied heavily on Arius and other Christian heretics but his main theological principles in contemporary form were lifted from Seventh-day Adventism.

Closely related in certain basic principles and approaches to the Bible, the Seventh-day Adventists and the Witnesses differ on many other doctrines. Pastor Russell, for example, denied the divinity of Christ and the doctrine of the Trinity; the Adventists do not. The Pastor attached no particular significance to the Jewish Sabbath whereas the Seventh-day Adventists branded Sunday observers with the mark of the beast. Both sects proclaim the imminent end of the world and the importance of Armageddon but the Adventists never arrived at the Pastor's calculation placing 1914 as the end of the times of the Gentiles.

In their attitudes toward civil society, health and education, the Adventists display a far more progressive and cooperative philosophy than the Witnesses. Adventists in the United States alone operate 11 liberal arts colleges, a theological seminary, and a Class A medical school. Outside of the adult education programs in local Kingdom Halls, the Witnesses content themselves with short courses for missionaries and congregational overseers.

Adventists emphasize health reform, conduct 27 hospitals and clinics in this country and dozens more in foreign mission areas. Thousands of doctors, nurses and dentists have received their training at the College of Medical Evangelists at Loma Linda, California. Bodily health as such gets no particular emphasis in the New World Society. If anything, the emphasis is negative: Witnesses are told to shun blood transfusions, hypnosis, psychiatry.

Adventists shun secular involvement to some degree but they do vote, run for political office, serve as noncombatants in the armed forces (an Adventist corporal won the Congressional Medal of Honor for heroism on Okinawa). Adventists expect members to observe total abstinence, tithe their income, send their children to parochial schools, follow Old Testament dietary regulations regarding pork and shrimp; Witnesses do not.

Adventists support an army of paid pastors, doctors, teachers, and church administrators. In fact, one Adventist in 19 works full time for the church. The Witnesses rely on volunteer help except for the pioneers and Bethel workers. Like the Witnesses, the Adventists seem to look upon the Bible as mainly a prophetical work and some of their numerical conclusions rival the Watchtower for naïvete. With such computations the Adventists seek to prove that the Pope wears the wicked 666 on his tiara. Numerically the two sects claim approximately the same following in the Uinted States although world-wide the older Adventist church reports slightly more members than the Watchtower. If growth rates continue the Witnesses will soon overtake the Adventists in membership.

Actually the theological system closest to the present Watchtower is that of a tiny and curious sect known as the Christadelphians. They number no more than 15,000 members. Like Jehovah's Witnesses, they are both unitarian and adventist. They too reject the Trinity and the divinity of Jesus Christ. Only the righteous will win eternal life while the wicked are doomed to suffer annihilation. The Second Coming is imminent but the Christadelphians cherish a peculiar belief that the saints will be ruled for 1,000 years from a seat of divine government in the Land of Canaan.

The Christadelphians baptize believers by immersion, employ no salaried ministers, refuse to vote or serve in the armed forces or accept public office. They operate no schools except a handful of Bible institutes during the summer months. Dr. John Thomas, a native of England, founded the Christadelphians after disillusionment with the Disciples of Christ. The name "Christadelphians" was adopted during the Civil War. Despite the many similarities with Watchtower doctrine, there seems to be no evidence that Russell ever encountered the Christadelphians during his years of religious searching.

In his study of the Black Muslim movement Dr. C. Eric Lincoln reveals that the mysterious founder of the movement, W. D. Fard, used Judge Rutherford's books in his private instructions.[3] Fard interpreted 1914 as the end of the rule of the "white devils." This would usher in a period of 70 years of grace before the non-whites would take over rule of the world.[4] His version of the battle of Armageddon was a final conflict between the whites and the Black Men which would be fought out in North America.[5]

To forestall any further schisms such as the Dawn Bible Students Association and the Associated Bible Students, the Watchtower has taken a number of preventive measures. Today all books and pamphlets and *Watchtower* articles are published anonymously. An ambitious officer of the Society would find it difficult to build up a national or international following since most of them remain unknown to the rank and file.

Congregational government was terminated in 1938; Brooklyn can now replace any congregational servant who appears to be leaning toward heresy or rebellion. The sect has been centralized in much the same way as Mary Baker Eddy centralized her Christian Science Church in the Mother Church at Boston. All publications must bear Brooklyn imprimaturs; no independent publications are circulated; all lecturers are expected to follow outlines prepared at headquarters.

No one knows if the Watchtower will escape further schisms but such an eventuality seems unlikely. Nothing succeeds like success. The spectacular growth of the movement, especially during the past three decades, can be used to persuade the restless and inquiring that Jehovah God is blessing the present hierarchy and methods.

14. *Whither Witnesses?*

WHAT DOES THE FUTURE HOLD for the Watchtower Society? Will its spectacular membership gain continue? Will committed Witnesses of Jehovah who now number almost 1,000,000 one day be counted in the millions?

Unlike the Witness prognosticators, we cannot dip into the Books of Daniel or Revelation for the answers to these questions. We can only rely on observation and educated guesses.

Some world conditions which have been favorable to the growth of the sect will probably continue for the indefinite future. The Watchtower Society plays upon man's fear of wars, disorders, revolutions, natural disasters, all of which it interprets as foretastes of Armageddon. If more people meditated on the reality that both the United States and Soviet Russia now possess H-bombs 1,000 times more powerful than the bombs which leveled Hiroshima and Nagasaki, they might also be candidates for the Brooklyn cult. Most secular prophets see a continuing Cold War between East and West; such a stalemate under the Damocles sword of the Bomb prepares the soil for the Watchtower message. When

Pastor Russell began predicting the end of things in the 1870's he could be dismissed as one of a long parade of religious fanatics. Today the voices of doom are joined by those of scientists, political leaders, military experts.

As the world shrinks, communications deliver the crises of the nations to our breakfast tables, and the full complexity of mankind's problems all but overwhelms the average citizen, he may be tempted to throw up his hands in despair of any solution. To him the Society whispers that these problems will never be solved by any human effort. Only Jehovah God can resolve all these perplexities by unleashing the forces of good and evil in combat at the battle of Armageddon.

One situation which once facilitated the Society's expansion in Africa may soon turn into a liability. By eschewing any assistance from or alliance with secular governments, the Watchtower could present itself to the Africans as free from the taint of hated colonialism. But now that these African nations are achieving independence, they may look with less favor on a Brooklyn-centered, white-dominated organization which belittles nationalistic aims and urges its followers to boycott civic affairs. These infant nations may prefer citizens who will seek higher education, enter into community life, vote and run for office if qualified. They may want more than passive though law-abiding residents. A large bloc of men and women who call themselves aliens in their homeland may run into opposition from national leaders. Restriction on the spread of such a movement could be in the offing.

Likewise the Watchtower and all Christian missionary movements in Africa face the relentless southward push of Islam. Today missiologists report that Islam counts ten converts from paganism for each native who adopts Christianity. With a simpler theology and moral code and a willingness to tolerate African customs such as polygamy, Islam may halt the growth of Jehovah's Witnesses on that continent as well as that of Catholics and Protestants.

As for Asia, the Watchtower never made significant gains in any Asian country except the Philippines. The Witness colony in India stands at only 1,622, five times the number of Witnesses in 1950 but still miniscule. There are about the same number of Japanese Witnesses. The Society is blocked in efforts to work on the China mainland.

While giving all due credit to Knorr we should not overlook the growth of the Society under the 25-year Rutherford rule. The growth pattern during this period becomes distorted to some degree because of the political events in Germany which halted Watchtower expansion and subjected the Society to harassment and crippling regulations.

In 1928 we have seen that there were 9,755 Bible Students in Germany and only 6,000 in the United States. Nazi persecution and World War II stopped further growth so that by 1946 there were only 8,895 German Witnesses of Jehovah. But by 1942 Rutherford had been able to boost the United States membership tenfold to 62,179. In Canada the cult jumped from 998 members in 1928 to 7,364 in 1942. We can see therefore that Rutherford's provocative proselytizing methods did result in a 1,000 per cent increase in this country and more than 700 per cent in Canada between 1928 and 1942.

World-wide, the average annual increase was about 15 per cent during the 1930's, reaching 25 per cent around 1940. Since 1950 it has leveled off at approximately 10 per cent a year. Even since Knorr's administration took control the growth has been uneven. In 1944, for example, the sect gained only 2,247 members over the preceding year and in

1956 the *Yearbook* showed an actual drop in members from 642,929 to 640,347.

What Knorr recognized was that Judge Rutherford's special forte of provocation had won about all the members such tactics would win. It was time for a change and Knorr's idea was to substitute politeness for provocation.

Another undetermined factor in the future growth of the cult is whether it can maintain the present high level of zeal and enthusiasm. Most Witnesses today are fairly recent converts. Hardly any have grown up in Witness families or are able to trace their family religious history to Russell or even to Rutherford. The zeal of converts is a familiar phenomenon, whether the converts embrace Catholicism, Communism, Moral Re-Armament, Zen Buddhism or Jehovah's Witnesses. They, more than the born devotee, are likely to try to share their new experience with unbelievers. As adult converts they have entered the faith with their eyes open; old doctrines have seemed fresh and exciting to them. They can recall the feelings and objections which kept them from embracing the new faith sooner and can understand the psychology of the prospective convert.

Can today's Witness parents pass on this enthusiasm to their children? Their grandchildren? Can they, for that matter, keep up the sense of urgency and discovery which now impels them to spend every spare moment warning their neighbors of Armageddon's imminence? Will the younger generation in Witness homes throw themselves into the drudgery of door-to-door missionary work which absorbs their parents? Will they pass up a chance to get a college education to devote more time to their preaching? Will they keep the faith in mixed marriages with orthodox Christians? Time will tell.

For some years the sect attracted men and women who admired an organization which seemed to defy the established state and churches. These were the same forces which were persecuting them. The anarchist, the rebel, the anticlerical, found sympathy in the Kingdom Hall. But many of the conditions which would draw those with persecution complexes have disappeared.

By the start of the 1960's most of the legal battles had been won. Seldom do Witnesses get into difficulties with local authorities over their right to propagate their views. The Supreme Court by establishing these civil rights has also taken away some of the appeal of the sect. In time of peace the sect runs into few problems on the question of draft exemptions. About the only unfavorable publicity which now appears concerns blood transfusion cases. The value of outside pressures in cementing the bonds of the Jewish community have often been analyzed; something of the same analysis may hold true for Jehovah's Witnesses. Without active persecution the sect fails to attract its share of the paranoic convert. The disgruntled Negro in Harlem may now look to the Black Muslims as a more vigorous protest than the predominantly white Watchtower.

Unlike the isolated communities of Amish or Mennonites or the older Mormon settlements in the West, the Witnesses live in cities and towns with non-Witness majorities. Witness children attend public elementary and high schools. Can these young people maintain their special views regarding the state, military service, higher education, evolution, orthodox religion, the United Nations and the like without some dilution, some compromise?

The Watchtower puts no particular emphasis on fertility. Unlike the Roman Catholics and Mormons, the Society should not expect any significant growth via the cradle. Witness families do not seem to be distinguished by their size. The Society sometimes counsels postponement of marriage until after Armageddon so that Witnesses can devote themselves wholeheartedly to their preaching work.

We have seen that the Society is already in the early stages of transformation from a sect to a church. Congregations are leaving rented quarters and building their own Kingdom Halls. Pioneers and circuit servants assume the duties carried on by full-time personnel and bishops in traditional churches. More converts with high-school and occasionally college diplomas present themselves for baptism. The loose congregational system was replaced in 1938 by the centralized theocratic form of polity. Brooklyn puts increasing emphasis on formal training at Gilead and through various short courses. Articles of a more or less sophisticated nature appear in the pages of the *Watchtower* and *Awake!* Old-time Witnesses might consider them highfalutin or worldly.

This gradual shift to church status becomes a mixed blessing because the sect has typically appealed to certain elements of society who do not feel comfortable in the more sedate atmosphere of the church. Some sects-turned-church exchange a measure of vigor and exuberance for white collars and B.A. degrees. Generally speaking, the more formal their education, the higher their salary bracket and social scale, the less willing the members will be to tramp around seeking converts.

The possibility of further schisms in the Watchtower cannot be altogether discounted. Already a dozen Russellite bodies propagate what they consider to be pure and ancient Russellism. The transfer of power from Rutherford to Knorr was far smoother than the earlier transfer and the cult has taken steps to stamp out any cult of personality. This does not mean that personality differences and ambition might not disrupt the next transfer. Overseas branches, especially in Africa, caught in the intoxication of new-found independence and national spirit, may yet prove troublesome to the Brooklyn hierarchy.

In the United States the attraction of Jehovah's Witnesses for the Negro, the Puerto Rican and Mexican-American may wane. By joining the Watchtower many people in these lower socio-economic classes may realize that they have taken a step which removes them even farther from the mainstream of American society. The Society provides no incentive for further secular education or professional advancement. Radical black supremacy cults such as the Black Muslims can make a stronger pitch to those who want to resign from society than the Watchtower can. Most Negroes seek greater integration into American society rather than withdrawal. They no longer wish to remain content with second-class citizenship. But Ferguson writes:

> Russellism is the religion of the consciously second-rate. Despite all its economical printing and the efforts of its enterprising founder, it would never have gained so strong a hold had it not been for the underdog's superb sympathy with himself.[1]

In recent years a fertile field for Witness missionaries has been disaffected Roman Catholics, especially those of the newer immigrations. Many Italians, Poles and other immigrants from southern and eastern Europe have felt uncomfortable in Irish-dominated parishes under Irish bishops and have drifted into the category of nominal or lapsed Catholics.

The picture of American Catholicism is changing rapidly. Fewer Roman Catholics will be found in the lowest economic class and many have reached or started the climb to social and professional status. A Roman Catholic sits in the White House. National parishes tend to lose their special ethnic identity and the old feuds among Catholics of differing nationalities are dying. The Catholic church accomplished the task of building churches and parochial schools, organizing diocesan institutions, founding colleges and hospitals, and pacifying conflicting nationalistic interests with only one serious schism: the 270,000-member Polish National Catholic Church.

Any observer of the religious scene will see a quickening of religious life in American Catholicism. Many parishes now organize Bible and discussion groups, encourage active participation and congregational singing at Mass, sponsor closed retreats for the laity, use laymen in a variety of positions such as foreign missionary once reserved to the priest and religious. New movements such as the Christian Family Movement, Legion of Mary, and Confraternity of Christian Doctrine deepen the spiritual life of Catholics and produce a better-informed laity. Liturgists even predict a wider use of English in place of Latin for worship, including the Mass itself; a number of ex-Catholics who have joined the Watchtower say they never knew what was going on at Mass since they knew no Latin. These developments taken together do not encourage the Witness proselytizer, since the number of marginal Roman Catholics with nationalistic frustrations seems to be declining.

The parish bulletin of Saint-Roch Church in Paris suggests some reasons why Catholics still join the Watchtower:

Why do people become Jehovah's Witnesses? Three factors contribute—the discovery of warm and brotherly communities;

the discovery of the Bible; the discovery of lively preaching easily understood by all. If they had found these things here, they would not have looked elsewhere.

Protestantism also seems to be undergoing a revival, marked especially by a concern for ecumenical efforts at closer cooperation, if not eventual reunion. This trend toward interfaith cooperation and actual merger of churches shows no signs of slowing down. The Witnesses do not see their sect as one more denomination; they ridicule the fragmentation of orthodox Christianity and the rivalries among churches and sects as evidence of Satanic influence. To many Protestants the cavalier attitude of the Watchtower toward mankind's problems is nothing but blasphemy. Commenting on the 1958 New York assembly, the leading Protestant interdenominational journal, the *Christian Century,* editorialized:

> Let those who will laugh off the whole phenomenon. For others the thought of 719,000 sectaries turning the Bible into a crystal ball, putting God on a schedule, trapping the Eternal in a timetable, is impious scandal. Ridiculing men's pathetic best efforts to make order in the earth is not faithful judgment but callous inhumanity. Being eager to leave "this worry-filled, problem-racked, loveless old world" is not humble piety but blasphemy, the back of men's hand in the teeth of the Almighty who is not only the hope of the next world but the Creator of this one.[2]

If, for the sake of discussion, we assume that the Watchtower prophets are wrong on their prediction of Armageddon, we must observe that the cult faces some genuine doctrinal crises during the next 20 years. Pastor Russell did not seem to learn the lesson of William Miller, adventist trailblazer, who predicted the end of the world in 1843 or 1844. Russell picked 1914 and lived to see the fateful year come and go without the overthrow of the Gentiles. The Watchtower Society today goes out of its way to avoid giving any precise date for the start of Armageddon. However the cult is committed to the dogma that the battle will begin during the lifetime of the generation alive in 1914. The average Witness seems to believe that Armageddon will certainly take place sometime before 1972. What will happen in 1973, in 1980, in 2000?

Actually, drawing on the experience of both the Watchtower and similar cults, we have a pretty good idea of what will happen if and when Armageddon does not materialize and the term "generation" can hardly be stretched any longer. A few Witnesses will give up the movement in disgust and disappointment. But the majority will no doubt accept whatever revised interpretation the Society's theologians devise to meet the situation. By the year 2000 the *Watchtower* may be speaking about the invisible Armageddon that took place years before. The whole timetable might be revised to conform to new readings of scriptural passages. But will such tortuous reinterpretations be able to spark the same fire and urgency which animates hundreds of thousands of Witnesses today?

Professor Joseph Bram of New York University states: "It is also legitimate to believe that, with the march of time, successive generations of Jehovah's Witnesses will make peace with the world (the French call this process *s'embourgeoiser*) and will give their prophecies a more symbolic and a less immediate connotation." [3]

A. Leland Jamison in the recently published study *The Shaping of American Religion* makes a similar observation:

> The astounding growth of the sect, together with the obvious prosperity of its members, leads some observers to surmise that it has already begun the evolution into denominational status. If the confidently voiced predictions of the climactic struggle at Armageddon within the next two decades are disappointed, the process of accommodation to the orthodox pattern may be accelerated. If one may look to the past for a model, the primitive Christian community, ardently apocalyptic at the outset, almost unconsciously developed the *modus vivendi* of the Catholic cultus, theology, and discipline in response to the frustration of the millennial hopes. It is not inconceivable that the Witnesses will follow suit.[4]

To refashion the traditional interpretations is no real problem for an organization such as the Watchtower. The cult puts no special emphasis on historical scholarship. No one, not even those in the training schools, is coaxed to study Russell or Rutherford and no one is likely to reprint Brother Knorr's books and speeches once he passes on to join the 144,000 anointed. Seminarians in traditional Christian churches study the writings of the Church Fathers, St. Thomas Aquinas, the Reformers who lived hundreds of years ago, but the Gilead student meets his scholastic requirements by mastering the current output of the Brooklyn presses. The Witness in the year 2000 will have as little occasion to read a 1962 issue of the *Watchtower* as a contemporary Witness has for studying Rutherford.

That the New World Society will suddenly run out of steam is doubtful. Whether Armageddon lies around the corner or not, hundreds of thousands if not millions of people live each day in the belief that it does. We would be as reckless as some date-setting Adventists if we tried to predict with any accuracy the effects of African and Asian nationalism, doctrinal reinterpretations, possible future schisms, administrative changes, and social upheaval on the flourishing Brooklyn cult.

APPENDIX A

Growth in Major Countries, 1918–1961
(The figures represent the average number of publishers (members) in these years)

Country	1918	1928	1938	1948	1958	1961
United States	743	6,040	25,596	72,945	202,141	248,681
Argentina	—	34	128	927	5,140	7,672
Australia	130	305	1,720	3,503	10,613	13,650
Austria	—	261	471	1,286	4,840	6,043
Belgium	—	—	117	1,177	4,933	6,366
Bolivia	—	22	47	109	289	407
Brazil	—	18	103	1,077	12,992	21,806
British Guiana	—	15	30	174	549	675
British Isles	2,784	3,066	4,959	14,676	37,416	44,974
Cameroun	—	—	—	—	3,239	4,570
Canada	—	998	3,113	12,603	30,933	36,459
Chile	—	—	26	191	1,433	2,380
Colombia	—	—	—	28	992	1,870
Republic of Congo	—	—	—	14	475	682
Costa Rica	73	—	—	637	2,034	2,386
Cuba	—	—	—	4,352	11,100	12,973
Cyprus	—	4	11	59	405	483
Dahomey	—	—	12	140	906	871
Denmark	26	324	889	3,260	8,638	9,372
Dominican Republic	—	—	—	128	274	617
Ecuador	—	—	—	29	354	691
El Salvador	—	—	—	—	429	591
Finland	—	305	429	2,610	6,859	8,011
France	—	447	845	2,627	11,094	15,655
Ghana	—	—	—	—	6,595	7,931
Greece	12	77	189	2,338	5,857	7,965
Guatemala	—	—	—	121	653	993
Haiti	—	—	—	36	430	786
Honduras	—	—	—	119	440	571

Country	1918	1928	1938	1948	1958	1961
India	2	69	291	267	1,222	1,622
Indonesia	—	—	—	—	262	477
Italy	—	—	—	329	4,248	5,838
Jamaica	50	84	390	1,465	3,814	4,324
Japan	—	75	110	—	978	1,876
Korea	—	—	—	—	2,532	3,914
Lebanon	—	—	—	—	453	610
Liberia	—	—	—	9	292	565
Mexico	—	—	309	4,711	15,623	22,235
Netherlands	—	57	234	4,190	10,158	12,007
Newfoundland	5	—	13	85	388	489
New Zealand	—	73	—	790	2,987	3,721
Nicaragua	—	—	—	72	280	414
Nigeria	—	7	427	5,511	22,926	31,195
Northern Rhodesia	—	—	939	9,873	25,669	27,988
Norway	15	85	328	992	2,946	3,455
Nyasaland	—	—	1,065	4,918	13,621	14,135
Panama	—	—	—	224	1,094	1,284
Peru	—	—	—	40	762	1,277
Philippines	—	—	—	3,589	23,355	29,190
Portugal	—	—	2	10	356	1,055
Puerto Rico	—	—	1	160	1,194	1,910
South Africa	—	58	378	4,440	14,451	17,416
Southern Rhodesia	—	—	323	3,599	11,810	11,949
Spain	—	—	—	34	894	2,011
Surinam	8	7	6	78	282	368
Sweden	—	253	982	3,231	7,464	8,412
Switzerland	—	763	813	1,660	4,168	4,932
Taiwan (Formosa)	—	—	—	—	1,429	1,900
Tanganyika	—	—	—	136	325	559
Thailand	—	—	1	48	267	343
Trinidad	—	189	—	980	1,439	1,552
UAR	—	—	14	96	421	443
Uruguay	—	—	4	249	1,005	1,458
Venezuela	—	—	—	51	1,410	2,314
West Germany	—	9,755	—	29,172	57,280	67,814
Iron Curtain countries					98,781	114,161
Other	20	597	1,828	24,357	8,449	13,243
Total	3,868	23,988	47,143	230,532	717,088	884,587

APPENDIX B

Annual Production of Books, Pamphlets and Magazines at Brooklyn Printing Plant
1936–1961

	Watchtower	*Golden Age, Consolation, Awake!*	Books and Pamphlets	Total
1936	1,548,150	3,233,800	16,683,051	21,465,001
1939	4,441,550	4,927,500	27,805,209	37,174,259
1942	9,922,640	6,642,390	19,617,951	36,182,981
1945	11,575,655	7,757,200	25,461,343	44,794,198
1946	14,559,150	10,683,200	15,684,381	40,926,731
1947	15,557,141	13,121,300	9,083,654	37,762,095
1948	14,701,250	12,439,900	18,395,370	45,536,520
1949	15,706,400	14,077,000	14,716,914	44,500,314
1950	18,038,800	16,493,600	10,549,195	45,081,595
1951	21,737,200	18,037,900	16,397,608	56,172,708
1952	26,135,600	19,999,824	12,657,919	58,793,343
1953	29,034,200	19,952,400	18,013,296	66,999,896
1954	33,858,200	23,538,610	20,015,380	77,412,190
1955	39,063,900	27,592,500	37,170,434	103,826,834
1956	49,307,350	34,425,109	19,186,124	102,918,583
1957	59,701,150	46,909,450	14,677,102	121,287,702
1958	68,840,840	55,527,425	17,063,326	141,431,511
1959	63,957,860	48,616,100	22,022,856	134,596,816
1960	57,402,520	47,935,500	20,066,806	125,404,826
1961	61,071,030	54,040,200	17,648,592	132,759,822

(The Society also prints its magazines, bibles and books in other printing plants around the world. In 1961 the total *Watchtower* production reached 95,296,708 copies and *Awake!* reached 88,969,505.)

APPENDIX C

The Three Corporations of Jehovah's Witnesses
(Chief offices and official address, 124 Columbia Heights,
Brooklyn 1, N. Y.)

First name	Date of incorporation	New names	Date of name change
Zion's Watch Tower Tract Society (Pennsylvania)	1884	Watch Tower Bible & Tract Society	1896
		Watch Tower Bible & Tract Society of Pennsylvania	1955
Peoples Pulpit Association (New York)	1909	Watchtower Bible and Tract Society, Inc.	1939
		Watchtower Bible & Tract Society of New York, Inc.	1955
International Bible Students Association (Great Britain)	1914		

BIBLIOGRAPHY

Algermissen, Konrad, *Christian Denominations.* St. Louis, B. Herder Book Co., 1945.

American Civil Liberties Union, *Jehovah's Witnesses and the War.* New York, American Civil Liberties Union, 1943.

—— *The Persecution of Jehovah's Witnesses. New York,* American Civil Liberties Union, 1941.

Awake!, semimonthly journal, various issues.

Axup, E. J., *The "Jehovah Witnesses" Unmasked.* New York, Greenwich, 1959.

Bach, Marcus, *They Have Found a Faith.* Indianapolis, Bobbs-Merrill, 1946.

Braden, Charles S., *These Also Believe.* New York, Macmillan, 1953.

Cole, Marley, *Jehovah's Witnesses: The New World Society.* New York, Vantage Press, 1955.

—— *Triumphant Kingdom.* New York, Criterion Press, 1957.

Cohn, Werner, *Jehovah's Witnessess as a Proletarian Sect.* New York, unpublished master's thesis at New School for Social Research, 1954.

Czatt, Milton Stacey, *International Bible Students.* New Haven, Conn., Yale University Press, 1933.

"Equipped for Every Good Work." Brooklyn, Watchtower Bible and Tract Society, 1946.

Ferguson, Charles F., *The Confusion of Tongues.* New York, Doubleday, Doran & Co., 1928.

From Paradise Lost to Paradise Regained. Brooklyn, Watchtower Bible and Tract Society, 1958.

Grigg, David H., *Do Jehovah's Witnesses and the Bible Agree?* New York, Vantage Press, 1958.

Hébert, Gérard, *Les Témoins de Jéhovah.* Montreal, Les Éditions Bellarmin, 1960.

Henschel, Milton G., "Who Are Jehovah's Witnesses?" Chapter in *A Guide to the Religions of America,* edited by Leo Rosten. New York, Simon and Schuster, 1955.

Jehovah's Witnesses in the Divine Purpose. Brooklyn, Watchtower Bible and Tract Society, 1959.

Knorr, Nathan Homer, "Jehovah's Witnesses" Chapter XXV in *Religion in the Twentieth Century,* edited by Vergilius Ferm. New York, Philosophical Library, 1948.

"Let God Be True." Brooklyn, Watchtower Bible and Tract Society, 1946.

"Let Your Name Be Sanctified." Brooklyn, Watchtower Bible and Tract Society, 1961.

Lockyer, Herbert, *Jehovah's Witnesses Exposed.* Grand Rapids, Mich., Zondervan Publishing House, 1954.

McKinney, George D., Jr., *The Theology of Jehovah's Witnesses.* Grand Rapids, Mich., Zondervan Publishing House, 1962.

Macmillan, A. H., *Faith on the March.* Englewood Cliffs, N. J., Prentice-Hall, 1957.

Martin, Walter R., and Klann, Norman H., *Jehovah of the Watch Tower.* Grand Rapids, Mich., Zondervan Publishing House, 1953.

Martin, Walter R., *Jehovah's Witnesses.* Grand Rapids, Mich., Zondervan Publishing House, 1957.

Mayer, F. E., *Jehovah's Witnesses.* St. Louis, Concordia Publishing House, 1943.

"New Heavens and a New Earth." Brooklyn, Watchtower Bible and Tract Society, 1953.

New World, The. Brooklyn, Watchtower Bible and Tract Society, 1942.

New World Translation of the Christian Greek Scriptures. Brooklyn, Watchtower Bible and Tract Society, 1950.

New World Translation of the Hebrew Scriptures. Brooklyn, Watchtower Bible and Tract Society, 1953, 1955, 1957, 1958, 1960.

Pike, Royston, *Jehovah's Witnesses.* New York, Philosophical Library, 1954.

Qualified to Be Ministers. Brooklyn, Watchtower Bible and Tract Society, 1955.

Quidam, Roger D., *The Doctrine of Jehovah's Witnesses, a Criticism.* New York, Philosophical Library, 1959.

Report of the 1958 Divine Will International Assembly of Jehovah's Witnesses. Brooklyn, Watchtower Bible and Tract Society, 1958.

Rosten, Leo, *A Guide to the Religions of America*. New York, Simon and Schuster, 1955.

Rutherford, Joseph F., *The Harp of God* (1921); *Comfort for the Jews* (1925); *Deliverance!* (1926); *Creation* (1927); *Government* (1928); *Reconciliation* (1928); *Prophecy* (1929); *Life* (1929); *Light,* two volumes (1930); *Vindication,* three volumes (1931); *Preservation* (1932); *Preparation* (1933); *Jehovah* (1934); *Riches* (1936); *Enemies* (1937); *Salvation* (1939); *Religion* (1940); *Children* (1941). Brooklyn, Watchtower Bible and Tract Society.

Russell, Charles T., *Studies in the Scriptures,* seven volumes: *The Divine Plan of the Ages* (1886); *The Time Is at Hand* (1889); *Thy Kingdom Come* (1891); *The Battle of Armageddon* (1897); *The At-one-ment Between God and Man* (1899); *The New Creation* (1904); *The Finished Mystery* (1917). Brooklyn, Watchtower Bible and Tract Society. Volumes I–VI published by Dawn Bible Students Association, East Rutherford, N. J.

—— *Tabernacle Shadows of the Better Sacrifices* (1881). East Rutherford, N. J., Dawn Bible Students Association, 1960 edition.

Schnell, William J., *Into the Light of Christianity*. Grand Rapids, Mich., Baker Book House, 1959.

—— *Thirty Years a Watch Tower Slave*. Grand Rapids, Mich., Baker Book House, 1956.

Stroup, Herbert H., *The Jehovah's Witnesses*. New York, Columbia University Press, 1945.

"The Kingdom Is at Hand." Brooklyn, Watchtower Bible and Tract Society, 1944.

Theocratic Aid to Kingdom Publishers. Brooklyn, Watchtower Bible and Tract Society, 1945.

"This Means Everlasting Life." Brooklyn, Watchtower Bible and Tract Society, 1950.

"Truth Shall Make You Free." Brooklyn, Watchtower Bible and Tract Society, 1943.

Van Baalen, J. K., *The Chaos of Cults*. Grand Rapids, Mich., Wm. B. Eerdmans Publishing Co., 1956.

Watchtower, The, semimonthly journal, various issues.

Whalen, William J., *Separated Brethren*. Milwaukee, Bruce Publishing Co., revised edition, 1961.

What Has Religion Done for Mankind? Brooklyn, Watchtower Bible and Tract Society, 1951.

Wilson, Bryan R., *Sects and Society*. Berkeley and Los Angeles, University of California Press, 1961.

Windle, Charles P., *The Rutherford Racket*. Chicago, Iconoclast Publishing Co., 1937.

1962 Yearbook of Jehovah's Witnesses. Brooklyn, Watchtower Bible and Tract Society, 1961.

You May Survive Armageddon Into God's New World. Brooklyn, Watchtower Bible and Tract Society, 1955.

"Your Will Be Done on Earth." Brooklyn, Watchtower Bible and Tract Society, 1958.

NOTES

CHAPTER 1

1. Charles W. Ferguson, *The Confusion of Tongues* (New York, Doubleday, Doran & Co., 1928), p. 64. Reprinted by permission of the publisher.

CHAPTER 2

1. Charles T. Russell, *The Atonement Between God and Man,* p. 354.
2. Charles T. Russell, *The New Creation,* p. 279.
3. Charles T. Russell, *The Divine Plan of the Ages,* p. 12.
4. *Ibid.,* p. 23.
5. *Ibid.,* p. 31.
6. *Ibid.,* p. 174.
7. *Ibid.,* p. 179.
8. *The New Creation,* p. 593.
9. *Ibid.,* p. 595.
10. Charles T. Russell, *The Time is at Hand,* p. viii.
11. A. H. Macmillan, *Faith on the March* (Englewood Cliffs, N. J., Prentice-Hall, 1957), p. 44.
12. Charles T. Russell, *Thy Kingdom Come,* pp. 314-315.
13. *Ibid.,* p. 317.
14. *Ibid.,* p. 326.
15. *Ibid.,* p. iii.
16. *Ibid.,* p. 163.
17. Bruce M. Metzger, "The Jehovah's Witnesses and Jesus Christ," *Theology Today,* April, 1953, p. 69.
18. *Watchtower,* Dec. 1, 1916, p. 374.
19. *Awake!,* May 8, 1951.
20. Ferguson, *op. cit.,* p. 71.

CHAPTER 3

1. *Watchtower,* March 1, 1961, p. 146.
2. *Jehovah's Witnesses in the Divine Purpose,* p. 68.

3. *Ibid.,* p. 69.
4. *Ibid.,* p. 72.
5. *Ibid.,* p. 91.
6. *Ibid.,* p. 105.
7. *Ibid.,* p. 133.

CHAPTER 4

1. Neil G. McCluskey, S.J., *Who are Jehovah's Witnesses?* (New York, America Press, 1956), p. 5.
2. *New World Translation of the Christian Greek Scriptures,* p. 25.
3. Bruce M. Metzger, "Review of New World Translation of the Christian Greek Scriptures," *Princeton Seminary Bulletin,* Spring, 1951, (v. 44:4), p. 59.
4. H. H. Rowley, "How Not to Translate the Bible," *The Expository Times, November,* 1953 (v. 65:2), pp. 41-42.
5. *Ibid.,* p. 42.

CHAPTER 5

1. *The Atonement Between God and Man,* p. 64.
2. Charles T. Russell, *The Unfinished Mystery,* p. 414.
3. Nathan H. Knorr, *Religion in the Twentieth Century,* Vergilius Ferm, ed. New York, Philosophical Library, 1948), p. 388.
4. *Eqiupped for Every Good Work,* p. 64.
5. *Let God Be True,* p. 68.
6. *Ibid.,* p. 74.
7. *Ibid.,* p. 75.
8. *From Paradise Lost to Paradise Regained,* p. 44.
9. *Ibid.,* p. 47.
10. *Ibid.,* pp. 64-65.
11. *Let God Be True,* p. 40.
12. J. F. Rutherford, *The Harp of God,* pp. 172-173.
13. *From Paradise Lost to Paradise Regained,* p. 168.
14. *Let God Be True,* p. 222.
15. *New Heavens and a New Earth,* p. 7.
16. *From Paradise Lost to Paradise Regained,* p. 205.
17. *Ibid.,* p. 211.
18. *Let God Be True,* p. 289.
19. *New Yorker,* June 16, 1956, p. 90, "I'd Like to Talk to You for a Minute," by Richard Harris.
20. *Let God Be True,* pp. 98, 99.
21. *Evolution Versus the New World* (1950), pp. 30-31.
22. *Ibid.,* p. 62.
23. *From Paradise Lost to Paradise Regained,* p. 126.

CHAPTER 6

1. *Watchtower,* April 1, 1960, p. 224.
2. *Watchtower,* June 1, 1961, p. 328.
3. *Qualified to Be Ministers,* p. 11.
4. *Ibid.,* p. 91.
5. *Ibid.,* p. 92.
6. *Ibid.,* p. 98.
7. *Ibid.,* p. 177.
8. *Ibid.,* p. 199.
9. *Ibid.,* p. 210.
10. *Watchtower,* May 1, 1961, p. 278.
11. *Qualified to Be Ministers,* p. 253.
12. *Ibid.,* p. 258.
13. *Watchtower,* June 15, 1961, p. 365.

CHAPTER 8

1. Albert Muller, "These Jehovah's Witnesses," *America,* June 24, 1961, p. 464.
2. *Ibid.,* p. 465.
3. *Watchtower,* Feb. 1, 1961, p. 92.
4. *The New York Times,* August 1, 1958.

CHAPTER 9

1. Eugen Kogon, *The Theory and Practice of Hell* (New York, Farrar, Straus and Co.), p. 43.
2. George N. Shuster, *Religion Behind the Iron Curtain* (New York, Macmillan, 1954), pp. 38-39.
3. *Awake!,* May 22, 1960, p. 12.
4. *Watchtower,* Nov. 15, 1960, p. 685.

CHAPTER 10

1. *Let God Be True,* p. 235.
2. *Ibid.,* p. 235.
3. *Ibid.,* p. 236.
4. *Ibid.,* p. 63.
5. *Ibid.,* pp. 257-258.
6. *The Time Is at Hand,* p. 346.
7. *Thy Kingdom Come,* p. 112.
8. Charles T. Russell, *The Battle of Armageddon,* p. x.
9. *The Kingdom Is at Hand,* p. 74.

10. *Ibid.*, p. 345.
11. *You May Survive Armageddon Into God's New World,* p. 52.
12. *Ibid.,* p. 155.
13. *Jehovah's Witnesses in the Divine Purpose,* p. 12.
14. *Qualified to Be Ministers,* p. 292.
15. *What Has Religion Done for Mankind?,* p. 272.
16. *Awake!,* Oct. 8, 1960, p. 14.
17. *Ibid.*
18. *Qualified to Be Ministers,* pp. 289-290.
19. *Awake!,* Jan. 8, 1961, p. 8.
20. *You May Survive Armageddon Into God's New World,* pp. 165-166.
21. *Let God Be True,* p. 86.
22. *What Has Religion Done for Mankind?,* p. 55.
23. *Ibid.*, pp. 16-17.

CHAPTER 11

1. Maximilian W. Kempner, "The Supreme Court and the Establishment and Free Exercise of Religion," *Religion and the Free Society* (Santa Barbara, Calif., Fund for the Republic, 1958), p. 68.
2. John E. Molder and Marvin Comisky, "Jehovah's Witnesses Mold Constitutional Law," *Bill of Rights Review,* Summer, 1942 (v. II, no. 4), p. 262.
3. Nathan H. Knorr, *op. cit.*, p. 391.

CHAPTER 12

1. Ferguson, *op. cit.,* p. 84.
2. *Ibid.,* p. 85.
3. *Make Sure of All Things,* p. 279.
4. *Watchtower,* Feb. 15, 1961, p. 128.
5. *Watchtower,* August 15, 1960, p. 507.
6. *Awake!,* Jan. 22, 1960, p. 28.
7. *Awake!,* March 8, 1960, p. 16.
8. *Watchtower,* Dec. 1, 1961, p. 735.
9. Leo Rosten, *A Guide to the Religions of America* (New York, Simon and Schuster, 1955), p. 63.
10. *Awake!,* March 8, 1960, p. 27.
11. Werner Cohn, *Jehovah's Witnesses as a Proletarian Sect* (New York, unpublished master's thesis at New School for Social Research), 1954, p. 34.
12. *Watchtower,* March 15, 1961, p. 185.
13. *Ibid.,* pp. 185-186.
14. *Watchtower,* Dec. 1, 1960, p. 728.

15. *Awake!,* April 22, 1953.
16. *Watchtower,* Dec. 1, 1960, p. 735.
17. McCluskey, *op. cit.,* pp. 15-16.

CHAPTER 13

1. *When Pastor Russell Died* (East Rutherford, N. J., Dawn Bible Students, 1957), p. 13.
2. *The Grace of Jehovah* (East Rutherford, N. J., Drawn Bible Students, 1955), p. 61.
3. C. Eric Lincoln, *The Black Muslims in America* (Boston, Beacon Press, 1961), p. 13.
4. *Ibid.,* p. 77.
5. *Ibid.,* p. 205.

CHAPTER 14

1. Ferguson, *op. cit.,* p. 88.
2. *Christian Century,* August 20, 1958, p. 942. Copyright 1958 Christian Century Foundation. Reprinted by permission from *The Christain Century.*
3. *Proceedings, New York Academy of Sciences,* October, 1956.
4. A. Leland Jamison, "Religions on the Perimeter," in James Ward Smith and A. Leland Jamison, editors, *The Shaping of American Religion* (Princeton, N.J., Princeton University Press, 1961), p. 206.

Index